The Latin language is popularly imagined in a number of specific ways: as a masculine language, an imperial language, a classical language, a dead language. This book considers the sources of these metaphors and analyzes their effect on how Latin literature is read. It argues that these metaphors have become *idées fixes* not only in the popular imagination but in the formation of Latin studies as a professional discipline. By reading with and more commonly against these metaphors, the book offers a different view of Latin as a language and as a vehicle for cultural practice. The argument ranges over a variety of texts in Latin and texts about Latin produced by many different sorts of writers from antiquity to the twentieth century. The author's central aim is to provoke more new readings that would both extend and complicate those that it offers, in order to catalyze revisionist thinking about Latin texts of all periods and about the general contours of the discipline of Latin studies.

JOSEPH FARRELL is Professor of Classical Studies at the University of Pennsylvania. He is the author of *Vergil's* Georgics *and the Traditions of Ancient Epic* (1991) and of papers on classical literature and culture. He is the director of The Vergil Project (http://vergil.classics.upenn.edu) and editor of *Vergilius*.

ROMAN LITERATURE
AND ITS CONTEXTS

Latin Language and Latin Culture

ROMAN LITERATURE
AND ITS CONTEXTS

Series editors
Denis Feeney and Stephen Hinds

This series promotes approaches to Roman literature which are open to dialogue with current work in other areas of the classics, and in the humanities at large. The pursuit of contacts with cognate fields such as social history, anthropology, history of thought, linguistics and literary theory is in the best traditions of classical scholarship: the study of Roman literature, no less than Greek, has much to gain from engaging with these other contexts and intellectual traditions. The series offers a forum in which readers of Latin texts can sharpen their readings by placing them in broader and better-defined contexts, and in which other classicists and humanists can explore the general or particular implications of their work for readers of Latin texts. The books all constitute original and innovative research and are envisaged as suggestive essays whose aim is to stimulate debate.

Other books in the series

Latin Language and Latin Culture

from ancient to modern times

Joseph Farrell

University of Pennsylvania

PUBLISHED BY THE PRESS SYNDICATE OF THE UNIVERSITY OF CAMBRIDGE
The Pitt Building, Trumpington Street, Cambridge, United Kingdom

CAMBRIDGE UNIVERSITY PRESS
The Edinburgh Building, Cambridge CB2 2RU, UK   www.cup.cam.ac.uk
40 West 20th Street, New York, NY 10011–4211, USA   www.cup.org
10 Stamford Road, Oakleigh, Melbourne 3166, Australia
Ruiz de Alarcón 13, 28014 Madrid, Spain

First published 2001

Transferred to digital printing 2002

Typeset in $9\frac{1}{2}$/12 Times New Roman and New Hellenic Greek on '3B2' [AO]

A catalogue record for this book is available from the British Library

ISBN 0 521 77223 0 hardback
ISBN 0 521 77663 5 paperback

For Ann, Flannery, and Kai

Contents

Preface

I would like to have written this book in Latin. On the other hand, had it been reasonable to do so – if such a book could have found an audience; if any publisher would have taken it on; if indeed I had full confidence that what I wanted to say could be expressed in a modern, idiomatic Latin style, supple and nuanced, not the stuff of composition exercises, critical editions, and public monuments – I would probably have seen no need to write it.

I offer this essay in the belief that certain ideas about the Latin language pervade modern intellectual life and color the ways in which most of us latinists carry out our professional responsibilities of teaching and research. These ideas affect us whether we work in antiquity, the Middle Ages, the Renaissance, or more recent times; whether we study literature, history, or any other area; whether the language itself is central or peripheral to our concerns. They include the idea of the "dead" language; the closely related idea of the "classical" language; the strong association between latinity and male speech; the structuring of the various disciplines within which latinists work according to discrete chronological periods; the relationship between the language itself and a multitude of social institutions, religious and secular, at different times, in different places. It is inevitable that these factors should influence the ways in which nonlatinists think about the most familiar of all ancient tongues; equally inevitable, perhaps, that such beliefs should affect the ways in which we latinists work as well.

At the same time, unexamined assumptions can have unexpected and unintended effects. For instance, I cannot imagine that many non-latinists, if they think about it, doubt that Latin is a masculine language. Of course, very few latinists today would openly endorse this idea; but it runs strong through the history of thinking about the language, and is therefore deeply ingrained in the institutional culture of latinity. For such reasons it influences the latinist's work and is worthy of frank examination and discussion. One point I shall argue is that the gender of the language itself takes on a different appearance when classicists and medievalists look across disciplinary boundaries at one another's material: how one thinks about the gender of Latin turns out to be deeply implicated in assumptions about periodicity. Similar relationships exist among the other beliefs listed above, and no doubt among many more that I have either failed to identify or did not feel able to handle adequately. Hence this book and, I hope, other books by other latinists on related themes.

My training is that of a classicist and a pretty conventional one at that. Virtually all my work to date has taken me down the most well-traveled paths over the most canonical terrain. My ulterior motive in writing this book was to create an excuse to roam around in neighborhoods that I had seldom visited and, in some cases, had only heard of. I am all too conscious that there are others much better qualified than myself to explicate authors like Perpetua, Venantius, Ekkehard, Dante, Woolf, and Stravinsky. I therefore address myself in the first instance, I suppose, to fellow classicists about the pleasures that come from straying outside the syllabus. Again I realize that many colleagues have been there before. From all who know these areas better than I let me beg their indulgence and offer this excuse: I wrote because no one else had come forward. My general idea, simply stated, is that all latinists, especially classicists, and especially those of us who are accustomed to working in the most familiar areas of Latin studies, should not only get out more often, but should make excursions to adjacent areas a more regular part of our work. Classicists owe a heavy debt to students of later periods, such as Ralph Hexter, Christopher Baswell, Thomas Greene, David Quint, Leonard Barkan, Susanne Wofford, and Michael Murrin, whose work goes far beyond treating antiquity as the raw material with which later ages had to work, but presents fresh and important perspectives on classical literature. Charles Martindale and Philip Hardie are perhaps the most prominent classicists who have taken seriously the need to read ancient texts in terms of their reception. But much more work remains to be done. Thinking about latinity just as a very small collection of familiar, world-class texts mostly produced at Rome over a relatively brief span of time by elite pagan men writing in the most rarified dialect of what is now a long-dead language, is neither an inevitable nor a preferable perspective. It is in fact more realistic to think of latinity as a vast and largely unexplored region of linguistic and social pluralism extending from remotest antiquity *down to the present day*. I would even suggest that, because this conception of latinity does extend to our own day, we who are interested in it might give more thought to the ways in which our discipline resembles a culture, and thus regard our studies not as the contemplation of a completely external, independent, objective reality but as a hermeneutic engagement with a developing entity in which we ourselves are inextricably involved.

So much for explanations; now on to the more pleasant task of giving thanks. The early stages of research and writing took place during a sabbatical leave supported by the University of Pennsylvania. The inordinate pleasures I have experienced in making this book have come not only from engagement with some wonderful material, but from the opportunity to work with and learn from many delightful individuals. To my colleagues and students in the Department of Classical Studies at Penn, my gratitude for their contributions to a rich and stimulating intellectual environment. Particular thanks to Jim O'Donnell, who read and commented on a draft of the entire book and, at a crucial early stage, downloaded what seemed like an enormous portion of his vast knowledge about topics in which I was and remain a mere novice. In addition to practical help, this experience inculcated a much better understanding of just what I was getting myself into, along with an extra measure of humility and respect for the subject. Several others have read parts of the book in draft or have fielded specific questions and discussed individual points, some very briefly, some at length, but all to good effect; these include Anna Morpurgo Davies, Judith P. Hallett, Cristle Collins Judd, Robert Kaster, Maud McInerney, James J. O'Hara, Donald Ringe, Joseph Schork. The example of those whose works have previously appeared in this series provided inspiration and a standard that I have tried to meet and uphold. My best thanks to the series editors whose vision provided a forum for this essay, and whose uncanny combination of learning, judgment, enthusiasm, and encouragement did so much both to launch and sustain the project and to improve it at many stages along the road to completion. The result would probably have been better if I had simply followed slavishly the advice of all these friends and helpers; for what blemishes remain, the responsibility is mine.

Finally, it is a pleasure to amplify the record, entered on the dedication page, of a more personal debt: to my wife, Ann de Forest, and also to my daughter, Flannery, and my son, Kai. All three of them helped shape the book, always for the better; and without them, it would probably not have been worth writing at all, in English, Latin, or any language.

Philadelphia, 1999

The nature of Latin culture

Coming to Latin culture

At the end of Virgil's *Aeneid* there occurs an episode in which the goddess Juno finally agrees to stop fighting. Her position, however, is far from abject. Speaking to Jupiter and sounding more like a conquering general than the patron of a defeated people, she dictates the conditions under which she will stop opposing the Trojan effort to settle in Italy. The native Latins must not change their ancient name, or become Trojans, or be called Teucrians, or alter their speech or dress. Their country should keep the name of Latium and be ruled by Alban kings forever. The strength of their Roman offspring should consist in their Italian manhood. Troy, having fallen, should remain fallen, even to the memory of its name. Jupiter readily accepts these terms, assuring Juno that "The people of Ausonia will keep their ancestral speech and culture, their name be as it was. Sharing bloodlines only, the Teucrians will subside ..." (12.823–36).

This Virgilian episode enacts a central Latin myth – a myth that concerns the power of latinity to establish its sway over non-Latins. Throughout history this power has been linked to the role of Latin as a civilizing force: an instrument for ordering the disorderly, standardizing the multiform, correcting or silencing the inarticulate. In these essays I shall explore this myth and other myths that have grown up around latinity or become attached to it throughout its long history. This exploration will take us into some areas where many readers, medievalists and neolatinists, will be more at home than I, and into others that, if not entirely unfamiliar, are seldom thought of as the home turf of any latinist. The Virgilian myth, I suspect, will be familiar to anyone who has been curious enough to pick up the book and read even this far. But if it is unfamiliar, no matter. This is a tale of initiation, and new initiates are always welcome.

The "universality" of Latin culture

The *Aeneid* is a foundational text. It tells about the beginning of Latin culture. When Juno stipulates what character this culture is to have, she speaks hardly at all of governmental forms or religious institutions, but of the most ordinary, and yet enduring aspects of daily life: what people wear, what they call themselves, and, most important for our purposes, what language they speak. Despite or because of this focus on the quotidian, Virgil represents Latin culture as almost monstrously potent, capable (through Juno's sponsorship) even in defeat of absorbing and occluding other cultures – here, especially, that of Troy. Just as Ascanius must change his name and become Iulus, founder of the Julian clan, so must Aeneas' followers put aside their Trojan language and customs so that their descendants, if not they themselves, may become fully Latin.

This seems to be how Virgil and his contemporaries regarded Latin culture, and later ages have tended to follow suit. For much of its history, latinity has been seen as a powerful weapon in Rome's arsenal, an instrument, in Virgil's words again, of sparing the conquered, warring down the proud. From a modern perspective, the idea of Latin as *the* imperial culture par excellence is widespread, and is constantly linked to the civilizing agency of the language itself. This idea was eloquently expressed by Edward Gibbon, who wrote,

> So sensible were the Romans of the influence of language over national manners, that it was their most serious care to extend, with the progress of their arms, the use of the Latin tongue. The ancient dialects of Italy, the Sabine, the Etruscan, and the Venetian, sunk into oblivion ... The western countries were civilized by the same hands which subdued them. As soon as the barbarians were reconciled to obedience, their minds were opened to any new impressions of knowledge and politeness. The language of Virgil and Cicero,

though with some inevitable mixture of corruption, was so universally adopted in Africa, Spain, Gaul, Britain, and Pannonia, that the
faint traces of the Punic or Celtic idioms were preserved only in the
mountains, or among the peasants.[1]

The policy is also attested in our ancient sources. Roman officials were
expected to use Latin in their dealings with alien peoples; some thought
that allowing even Greek to be spoken in the Senate bordered on
the scandalous. Eventually, even in such a center of Greek culture as
Antioch, Libanius would complain about the necessity of knowing
Latin.[2]

If Virgil celebrates the moment when it was settled that Latin would
be spoken at Rome, other poets were happy to represent the language's
extension throughout the world as a vehicle for their poetry. Ovid predicts that his masterpiece, the *Metamorphoses*, "will be recited wherever
Roman power extends over conquered lands" (15.877). Martial, too,
revels in the idea that his poetry is read throughout the empire (traveling, often enough, along with the army); but it is in the capital that he
finds the strongest symbolic contrast between Latin and barbarian
speech. Martial celebrates the emperor Titus' dedication of the Colos-
seum by speaking of the immense arena as encompassing the entire
world: "What race," the poet asks, "is so remote, so barbarous, Caesar,
that no spectator from it is present in your city?" (*Spect.* 3.1–2).
Moving around the circle of the great amphitheater, he catalogues the
races represented there in a way that conducts the reader on a geographical circuit of the empire: Sicambrians and Thracians from the
north; Sarmatians, Cilicians, Arabs, and Sabaeans from north to south
in the east, Egyptians and Ethiopians to the south; and the dwellers
along the shores of Ocean in the west (3–10). All of these peoples are
distinguished by their different customs and characteristics, or by the
exotic products of the lands they inhabit. But the poem, like the circuit
of empire that it describes, also moves in a ring: the point of *barbara* in

---

[1] Gibbon (1909–14), 1.41. Gibbon's position is upheld by linguist Jorma Kaimio,
who writes that, to prove that the Romans followed a definite language policy, "it
is only necessary to point to a linguistic map of modern Europe." Kaimio (1979),
327.

[2] Libanius, *Orat.* 1.234, 255.

line 1 is finally brought home at poem's end as Martial caps the theme of diversity by turning to the matter of speech:

Vox diversa sonat populorum, tum tamen una est,
    cum verus patriae diceris esse pater.

These peoples speak in different voices, then with one, when you are
called true father of your country.   *Spect.* 3.11–12

Foreign speech is thus acknowledged, but is represented as multiform, inarticulate, and confused – *diversa* (11). Against this babbling, Martial allows the crowd one intelligible utterance in the one language that could render them intelligible: the poem concludes with the hailing of the emperor, in Latin, by that characteristically Roman and national-istic title *pater patriae*. The barbarian crowd thus reenacts in speech their own political subjugation by Titus and by Rome.

The effects of Roman linguistic imperialism were real. On the other hand, ancient and modern beliefs about the power of Latin are based on ideological constructs, not universally valid, objective truth. We know for instance that Latin culture took firm root in the west; but Gibbon, in the passage I have cited, goes on to observe what everyone knows, that failure to establish Latin in the eastern provinces was an important factor that led to the eventual disintegration of the empire. What he does not say is that this failure betrays as wishful thinking the imperi-alist claims of Latin culture generally, as well as the basic fictiveness of these claims. Stories emphasizing this fictiveness tend to be less often told than the imperialist kind rehearsed above. This is unfortunate on two counts. First, these "other stories" are interesting in themselves. Second, and paradoxically, the wishful, triumphalist tales about an all-powerful linguistic and cultural force may actually have contributed to the marginalization of latinity within modern intellectual discourse, and to the perception that Latin is, or wants to be, everything that a modern language is not: that it is the paradigmatic "dead language."

What "other stories" does Latin culture have to tell? If latinity was no monolith, even in its ancient capital, it was certainly subject to the same pressures as the languages that it encountered along the permeable cultural frontier. The case of Ovid is instructive. When official displea-sure relegated him to the very limit of the empire, he got the opportu-nity to reflect on his earlier boast that he would be recited "wherever

Roman power extends." Writing in his exile poetry about conditions at Getic Tomi, he returns over and over to the absurdity of composing or even thinking in Latin so far from Rome, suggesting that removal from the native seat of Latin culture has actually weakened his grasp on the language. We need not take this claim seriously to believe in the anxiety on which it depends. Against the Virgilian model of universal extension and absolute potency we can set the countervailing Ovidian model of an outpost culture barely maintaining a degree of integrity against a much more powerful and numerous barbarian Other. The exilic myth, in fact, is the story that was told more often and more openly as Latin political power waned and the language itself was left as the chief embodiment of the culture that survived, eventually becoming virtually coterminous with it.

Ovid's excursion to the spatial limits of empire anticipates later developments along the axis of time. With political change came cultural evolution, facts that are reflected with clarity in the mirror of language. By late antiquity, Christian policy makers were vigorously debating whether to observe classical pagan usage or to cultivate a distinctively pietistic latinity. Centuries later the British courtier Alcuin considered the Latin spoken and written in Charlemagne's realm so corrupt that he instituted a thoroughgoing reform of orthography and pronunciation, and thus played a role, possibly a decisive one, in distinguishing Latin from the Romance languages. The Renaissance humanists fought over the question of whether modern Latin should be based exclusively on a ciceronian model. Examples could be multiplied, but the point is clear. Latin culture tends to imagine itself and its language as universal and powerful beyond all competitors. It constructs an image of the Latin language as possessing similar qualities, along with definite canons of correctness conferring a stability that other languages lack. Though the language does change, these canons remain, and the history of latinity is marked by various "renascences" during which the language is "reformed" on an ancient, "classical" model. Of course, "reform" always involves the rejection as "vulgar," "rustic," "provincial," "late," "ecclesiastical," "medieval," "effeminate," or simply as "barbaric," of linguistic habits and protocols that do not conform to the proposed standard. It is as if not power, but anxiety about its ability to resist the forces of linguistic "debasement," drove Latin culture to marginalize the linguistic Other and to claim an overweening potency and value for itself. But ultimately, latinity has become a victim of its own success. By promulgating and subscribing to a relatively one-dimensional linguistic caricature, Latin culture – and particularly the classicizing element of that culture – has paid the price for cutting itself off from sources of diversity and energy that might have ensured a more vibrant state of health.

Latin culture in the modern world

The *Aeneid* is, of course, famously untranslatable. The episode cited above in which Juno delivers her terms of "surrender," lacks when read in English or indeed any language other than Latin, much of its effect – but for a reason that, in this case at least, has nothing to do with Virgil's celebrated mastery of Latin as an expressive medium. Reading the passage in translation, one misses none of the semantic content. A deal has been cut. Its terms and its consequences are clear. It is the impact of the narrative event as much as any prosodic virtuosity that most impresses the reader.[3] But if one does read the episode in Latin, a whole range of additional responses comes into play.

What sort of responses? First, perhaps, there is the consciousness of employing a skill that has been acquired at some personal cost. For many, part of this cost is years of effort and submission to a pedagogical system in which the student must try every day to construe specimens of Latin under the watchful eye of a teacher who will respond by pointing out and discussing at length and in meticulous detail each and every one of the student's mistakes. This is a type of education that teaches humility as well as Latin and that equates humility with ignorance of Latin, pride with knowing it well. Understandably, few willingly put themselves through this process for long. Some, however, persist until one day they arrive at the end of the *Aeneid*. The sense of youthful accomplishment that might well attend any reader approaching the end of the epic in Latin for the first time is understandable, almost inevitable. Indeed, it can be expected to recall earlier sensations. I can still remember clearly how I felt when a teacher encouraged my classmates and me not to abandon Latin after the tedium of Caesar and Cicero, because after all that hard work we were poised to reap the rewards

---

[3] On this passage see Johnson (1976), 114–34, especially 124–27.

offered by Virgil. Some who took this advice lived to wonder about a reward that meant spending a semester or a year slogging through a few thousand lines of poetry parceled out in snippets that were truly minuscule compared to what they could handle in their own, or even in other, foreign languages. But to those who stuck it out, the accomplishment seemed all the greater. Simply reaching the end of the poem, having endured the tedium, the labor, and the seemingly endless deferral of gratification that this process entailed – for to the novice, the task seems truly heroic – even these apparently extraneous elements of the experience helped put the young reader in touch with the emotions Aeneas himself must have felt in his hour of glory.

Viewed from this perspective, the text of the *Aeneid* becomes not merely a narrative, but a kind of script for the establishment of Latin culture, a script that might support a limitless series of performances, each with its own variations, but all sharing certain crucial features. The series begins on the mythic level with the labors of the founder, Aeneas. It includes the political level and the establishment of stable government by the *princeps*, Augustus. And, I suggest, it extends to the education of the neophyte who by acquiring the skills necessary to read the national epic gains full membership in Latin culture.[4]

But what is the culture into which the young modern reader of the *Aeneid* is received? The culture of latinity is not the same thing as a hermeneutics of reception, not a sum total of "influences," direct and indirect, upon modern encounters with the latinity of the past.[5] It may indeed be related to this. But even more, it is the culture *embodied by* the language, to which all who study and value latinity belong. It is concerned in the first instance with the language itself: its character, its qualities, its capacities, its limitations. The business of learning Latin, reading Latin, studying and writing about Latin, even remembering (with whatever emotions) one's school Latin or thinking of the language only occasionally, is bound up in shared experiences, patterns of behavior, common rituals, and also in differences of opinion, parallel oppositions, persistent prejudices. To encounter Latin nowadays is to belong to this culture, which is larger and more heterogeneous than one might expect it to be. In fact, even now, as one looks back on a century

---

[4] On this aspect of Latin education in the Renaissance see Ong (1959).
[5] Important arguments about this problem in Martindale (1993).

that, judged superficially, has been fairly inhospitable to Latin studies as an institution, Latin culture is not in bad shape; for, while the language itself lies at the heart of this culture, ideas about the language are not confined to professional latinists. One of the beauties of this culture is that it is something to which latinists belong, but it is not something anyone can control. Most of all, it is something from which everyone can learn.

Just as social anthropologists have come to appreciate the unavailability of an objective vantage point on the contemporary, so, I would suggest, should Latin studies abandon any pretense to a disinterested perspective on a past culture that is wholly Other. Indeed, the latinist's implication in his or her "material" is much tighter than the anthropologist's or the ethnographer's. Visiting another culture, an investigator cannot help but have some impact on it, and frequently will attempt to assimilate it to the greatest extent possible, but always with the understanding that the process takes place across cultures that are, ultimately, strangers. The ethnographer's interest in and understanding of other cultures depends upon intervention; but those cultures exist independent of one's own. They may change as a result of the ethnographer's intervention, but they would continue to exist even without it. This is not true of Latin culture. The latinist cannot work by traveling to a foreign land. Access to the past is rooted in the here-and-now. The latinist's subject, unlike the ethnographer's, would not exist without the interest and activity of contemporary scholars, students, enthusiasts, dabblers, even opponents. In an important sense, then, Latin culture is a creature of the modern world. More than any anthropologist can be, we, too, are natives here.

Continuity and rupture

Nativism of course is an extremely complex issue in Latin culture, ancient or modern, and I shall return to it at the end of this chapter. Related to it is another problem raised by my reading of the *Aeneid* as an initiation rite. Juno's insistence that Aeneas' people become linguistically and culturally Latin, I suggested, draws a line from the hero himself through Augustus and then to generations of novices who by reading the poem prove themselves as Latins. This raises the question of continuity. Is the Latin culture to which I have referred perfectly continuous with that of the ancient Romans? I can easily imagine some readers, for various reasons, answering "No! Latin culture belonged to the ancient Romans, and it died with them. If there really *is* a 'modern Latin culture', it is not the same thing as, nor is it even continuous with, the culture of Roman antiquity." Fair enough; but the issue of continuity cannot be dismissed so easily. To put the matter in perspective, let me reply with a different question: if ancient Latin culture did indeed meet its end, when did this happen? The answer, I believe, is far from clear.

To get some purchase on this question, let us consider, what is a "latinist?" In theory, someone called a latinist might be a student of Hildegard, Petrarch, or Sweedenborg instead of Cicero or Virgil, and might make a professional home in a department of History, Philosophy, Religion, Comparative Literature, Romance Languages, or even English rather than in Classics. But for some reason, a person whose professional interests lie beyond antiquity will usually be called a "medievalist," a "comparatist," or something more descriptive (or differently descriptive) than "latinist" – which, as matters now stand, normally denotes the *classicist* who specializes in Latin. Such a latinist's area of expertise, as fixed by such documents as graduate school reading lists and histories of literature, extends little farther in time than Juvenal (†127?) or at any rate than Apuleius (†170?), Fronto (†175?), and Aulus Gellius (fl. 170), if we are speaking of authors; or, if we prefer to speak of more definite landmarks in political history, than the death of Marcus Aurelius (180). This is a particularly useful landmark because on July 17th of the same year there occurred at Carthage a hearing followed by the trial and execution of several people from the town of Scillum who were ordered to swear their loyalty by the Genius of the Emperor and to offer sacrifice for his health, but who refused on the grounds that they were Christians; and the text that informs us about this event, the *Acts of the Martyrs of Scillum*, is the earliest Christian text in Latin that we possess. The oldest Latin translations of the Bible are thought to date from this time as well. And it is from this point that Gibbon dates the "decline" that led inevitably to the "fall" of the Roman empire.

In any case, we are speaking of a process rather than an event. It was a long time before pagan culture lost its ascendancy to the new religion. If we insist on some sort of terminus, perhaps we should look for a more decisive event more firmly linked to the history of the language. What we are seeking may in fact be a nonevent: between the years 254 and 284, no Latin literature that we know of was produced, of *any* kind.[6] This is a remarkable, possibly unparalleled occurrence in the history of literature. The language continued to be spoken, of course; but since we have no real access to the spoken language, the conditions that made possible such a complete lapse in the production of "literature" appear as an actual tear in the fabric of Latin culture. After this disastrous period, new imperial administrative structures were created by new Augusti and a new senatorial aristocracy came on the scene to cultivate a classicizing literature of their own, while grammarians codified the language along classical models. But all of this activity could be motivated by nostalgia, even perhaps denial: by a desperate longing to resuscitate what was, in fact, a dead body.

These points on the timeline have an undeniable appeal, but it is difficult to trust them implicitly. Certainly there are authors on the modern side of this rupture who, like Servius and Macrobius, are valued partly because they are considered native speakers of a living Latin, and thus unlike ourselves. Still, one hardly thinks of them as breathing the same air as Cicero or Virgil. Rome was no longer the seat of power. The time was approaching when there would be no senatorial aristocracy to speak of. Claimants to the title "Augustus" persisted (the last one resigned in 1806); but in late antiquity, the most powerful person in the west came to be the king of the Franks, a people who coexisted in the same territories with the more Romanized Gauls. These Gauls cherished the idea that they were the true inheritors of Latin culture, and modern historians often dignify them with the name "Gallo-Roman." The Franks, or at least the Frankish court, aspired to this condition as well. Both groups were obsessed with a form of identity politics that has become all too familiar nowadays, and both coveted validation of the right to call themselves Roman, to see themselves as members of a living Latin culture.

Classical poets were in short supply in those days, but anyone who could function as such could make a good career for himself. Venantius Fortunatus, a young man born and raised in the Veneto, arrived in this

---

[6] On this rupture see O'Donnell (1994).

milieu not too long after the mid-sixth century.[7] In the preface to his collected poems, he announces himself, however playfully, as a second Orpheus, singing in the wilderness to barbarians. It is worth bearing this passage in mind when we read his praises of patrons such as the kings Charibert and Chilperic or the duke Lupus. These Frankish noblemen offered the poet patronage and preferment, and the man who arrived at the Burgundian court a wandering poet died Bishop of Poitiers. The native tongue of these noble patrons was Germanic: if Venantius was an ersatz Orpheus, they were authentic barbarians. But they aspired to membership in Latin culture, which by this time had become so much a matter of language that to a wandering poet fell the power to confer it upon them by writing conventional Latin panegyrics in their honor.

The forms taken by Venantius' praise are instructive. Descending from a long tradition of regal panegyric in prose and verse, they adapt tradition to current realities in telling ways. We have seen Martial praising Titus as singular ruler of the entire world by celebrating the occlusion of plural, inarticulate, barbarian languages by a universal latinity. Venantius invokes a similar motif in his encomium of Charibert, but with an important difference:

> Hinc cui Barbaries, illinc Romania plaudit:
> diversis linguis laus sonat una viri.

> On this side Barbary acclaims him, Rome on that: in different
> tongues sounds the man's unique praise.   *Carm.* 6.2.7–8

Here Latin does not occlude barbarian speech, but is forced to share the stage. Indeed, Latin voices explicitly take second place, as in a later passage that comments on the king's bilingual eloquence:

> Cum sis progenitus clara de gente Sigamber,
> floret in eloquio lingua Latina tuo;
> qualis es in propria docto sermone loquella,
> qui nos Romanos vincis in eloquio?

---

[7] Auerbach (1965) is dated but remains an important assessment of many of the problems with which we are concerned here, including Venantius' place in literary history. Godman (1987), 1–37, offers a stimulating defense and a challenging reading of Venantius' occasional poetry. For a more comprehensive introduction to the poet and his work see George (1992).

Though born a Sicambrian (of famous lineage), it is in *your* eloquence the Latin tongue flourishes; what must you be like in learned
speech in your native language, you who better us Romans in eloquence?   *Carm.* 6.2.97–100

Not only does Charibert outshine professional Latin rhetoricians like
Venantius, but he beats them at their own game, outdoing them in
Latin, leaving the poet – evidently not bilingual like his patron – to
wonder what a spellbinder the king must be in his native Germanic,
itself praised here as a medium of polished eloquence. In a related move,
Venantius combines these two motifs in his encomium of Chilperic,
Charibert's half-brother and dynastic rival:

Quid? quoscumque etiam regni dicione gubernas,
   doctior ingenio vincis et ore loquax,
discernens varias sub nullo interprete voces:
   et generum linguas unica lingua refert.

Why, whomever you govern under the sway of your kingship you
surpass, well-schooled of mind, eloquent of tongue, understanding
various languages with no interpreter: your tongue alone answers the
tongues of nations.   *Carm.* 9.1.91–94

And, in the same poem, the motif of the interpreter appears again to
provide a learned gloss on the king's name:

Chilperice potens, si interpres barbarus extet,
   "adiutor fortis," hoc quoque nomen habes:
non fuit in vacuum sic te vocitare parentes:
   praesagum hoc totum laudis et omen erat.

Mighty "Chilperic" – or, had we a barbarian interpreter, "Strong
Advocate" (for this is your name as well) – not in vain did your
parents call you thus: all this was a presage and an omen of your
fame.   *Carm.* 9.1.27–30

Once again the poet disavows personal knowledge of barbarian speech,
displacing authority for the learned bilingual etymology onto the absent
figure of the Frankish translator, skilled in Latin as well as Germanic.[8]

---

[8] For more on "Roman" and "barbarian" in Venantius see Szöverffy (1977).

Granting these diplomas of linguistic skill was not Venantius' most lasting or, perhaps, his proudest achievement. Not long after the poet's arrival in Burgundy he looked elsewhere, seeking the patronage of Radegund, former queen of Lothar I but since 544 the leader of a religious community at Poitiers. Radegund was at the time of Venantius' arrival in Gaul involved in a diplomatic effort to obtain a relic of the True Cross from the Byzantine emperor Justin II and the empress Sophia. To this end she enlisted the services of Venantius, who composed a trio of learned Latin poems to help make her case. The effort was successful and the relic was installed in 569; a fourth poem, a *gratiarum actio*, also survives. These along with the rest of Venantius' oeuvre are, rightly or wrongly, not much read or esteemed nowadays by most of those who identify themselves simply as "latinists." But two of his works, *Vexilla regis prodeunt* (2.6) and the exquisite *Pange lingua gloriosi* (2.2), both written to celebrate the installation of the relic at Poitiers, are still sung by thousands, perhaps millions, in their monodic settings as part of Holy Week observances in the Roman Catholic Church. They have been fairly widely recorded as well; several performances of them could be purchased today in any reasonably well-stocked record store. There would seem to be few artifacts of the ancient world of which anything like this can be said; and yet there are few that are considered less representative of Latin culture than these Christian hymns composed for a female patron of Germanic extraction living in a convent in Gaul. That Venantius' work should be denied a place in the canon of classical poetry is perhaps understandable. How vital was the language in which he wrote or the culture that he conferred on his barbarian and Christian patrons? We are forced to infer from the successful trajectory of his career that Venantius' patrons wanted to be praised in Latin, even as the poet repeatedly defers to Frankish cultural superiority. Nevertheless, the desire of the Frankish nobility for praise of this type is rather difficult to understand. Isn't such poetry in itself compelling evidence that latinity was already not merely dead, but a fossil?

Grammatical and vulgar speech

This commonly-held position remains surprisingly hard to establish. By the sixth century, the Latin language and Latin culture had reached the point at which scholars stop looking for the death of Latin and start searching for the birth of Romance. But the more we learn about medieval Europe, the more difficult it is to discern the moment when Latin dies and Romance is born.

To begin with, we do not know when the Franks, who began to occupy the Roman provinces of Europe from the fourth century on, adopted Latin and abandoned Germanic as their "native" language. Indeed, we do not know to what extent this is even an accurate model of what happened. Did they, in fact, abandon Germanic, or did the Franks consider both languages their own? Are we speaking of the nobility only, or did the phenomenon transcend distinctions of class? When did Latin begin to evolve into Romance, and how long did this process take? Did Latin survive as a written language long after the spoken language had ceased to be recognizable as such? Where it used to be assumed that the process whereby Latin became Romance took place at the latest during the seventh, eighth, and ninth centuries, it is now thought by some that two different languages cannot be clearly distinguished until two or more centuries later, and not finally distinguished even then.[9]

On one view, the distinction between Latin and Romance was the artificial creation of Alcuin's previously mentioned attempt under Charlemagne to reform the orthography and pronunciation of Latin on (what he thought was) a classical model. This argument rests partly on the notion that Alcuin, a Briton, would have come to Charlemagne's court speaking an insular Latin, a language different from the vernaculars that surrounded it, one that was taught to Britons very much as a foreign tongue constructed on conservative grammatical principles. Under such circumstances, one infers, Latin would have been more resistant to corruption than on the continent, where vernacular influence would have been inevitable. In his attempt to enforce a uniform standard of spelling and pronunciation, then – an attempt based on contemporary insular practice – Alcuin can be argued not to have restored classical Latin, which was his goal, but to have "invented" medieval

---

[9] This is an enormous, difficult, and much-debated topic fraught with problems related to nationalism and modernist ideology. Important contributions include: Bardy (1948); MacMullen (1966); Norberg (1966); Millar (1968); McKitterick (1989).

Latin as an artificial and mainly literary entity distinct from spoken Romance, which then developed into French, Spanish, Italian, and so forth.[10]

It is a good story. It may even be, in some sense, true. But true or not, it is a spectacular vehicle for thematic analysis. At issue in this as in other stories of Latin's demise is a strong element of teleology that appears to work like this: it is "known" that Latin is now a "dead" language, the exclusive preserve of academic specialists, unsupported by a living culture. The task is to discover when this situation first came about. One feels sure that this is in fact what happened, just as the Roman empire "fell," but the coroner's certificate contains a blank space labeled "date." Alcuin's reforms are as good an event as any on which to blame Latin's demise – which is to say, not very good at all. Long after Charlemagne, scholars, clerics, and diplomats throughout Europe continued to write and converse fluently in Latin, many of them perhaps exclusively or nearly so. That this can be said only of a cultural elite is true enough. But the same view can be taken of the rise of any official modern vernacular, such as Italian, which in its "official" form was spoken by only a tiny fraction of the total population of Italy until late in the last century.[11] It is further striking that we find in the story of Alcuin the pre-echo of a characteristic still operative in modern Latin culture. First, his classicizing objectives awaken the sympathies of the modern (classical) latinist, who sees in the presiding intelligence of the Carolingian "renascence" a kindred spirit. Second, though Alcuin did not "restore" latinity to its ancient form, by marking a boundary between classical and medieval Latin on the one hand, and between Latin and the vernacular on the other, he performs a service of great importance by ratifying linguistic and cultural categories that latinists hold dear. Third and last, it is significant that the individual credited with performing this service is figured as an interloper, the product of a culture in which Latin was already cultivated as a learned language so different from the vernacular as to be immune from contamination or confusion with it. The linguistic situation in Francia we imagine as much more fluid, so much so that we cannot draw a line between Latin and Romance. In Britain, we imagine that Latin existed only among certain social groups as a highly constructed idiom that had no rela-

---

[10] On this theory see Wright (1982).   [11] De Mauro (1972), 36–45.

tionship to or interaction with the vernacular; and it is therefore, paradoxically, the British arriviste who, appalled at the condition to which the language has descended among native speakers, sets things straight. What makes this story so intriguing is its resemblance to situations both in the ancient world, as when it fell to Greek slaves to organize and operate a system of education and a national literature for native speakers of Latin, and in the modern world, in which scholars raised speaking languages that are not descended from Latin have occasionally, in their own minds at least, tried to assume over speakers of the Romance languages a certain hegemony with respect to Latin studies. It is as if the status of the linguistic foreigner were actually an essential qualification for full membership in Latin culture.

Alcuin's example points out the crucial fact that one can hardly conceive of Latin as anything but an "other" language. Indeed, it is essentially impossible to point to a single specimen of Latin written at any time or place that can stand as a witness to the existence of a sincere, nativist Latin culture. In each period and every form through which Latin speaks, it has demonstrably internalized its "othered" status.

The most influential statement on this aspect of Latin is Dante Alighieri's essay *On Eloquence in the Vernacular*. In book I of this work, Dante divides all the world's languages into two categories: the natural, which are the original and more noble sort, and the "artificial" or "grammatical," which are later human constructs. In the former category he places the vernacular speech used every day in different forms in different places; in the latter such languages as, preeminently, Latin. His argument is remarkable in that Latin was in the late Middle Ages a language of great prestige as compared with the vernacular. Dante acknowledges this fact by referring to Latin's enormous utility as a "grammatical" language, one based on a rational system rather than on natural usage and thus impervious to change across time, national boundaries, or any similar factor. Latin for Dante is Latin, one and the same, always and everywhere. The vernacular, on the other hand, is capable of extensive and confusing variation over time and from place to place. Typically, he explains this property of natural language with reference to a Judeo-Christian view of history, tracing the mutability of natural language to God's punishment of humankind for constructing the Tower of Babel. The pristine state of the original human speech – probably some form of Hebrew – gave way to a degraded condition in a way that mirrors precisely the contrast between the Edenic and post-lapsarian conditions lived by the original humans Adam and Eve. Artificial language based on grammar is thus but a synthetic expedient, like clothing, a cultural institution that enables humankind to cope with the degraded life that is the wages of sin. But natural language, according to Dante, retains its inherent superiority and greater "nobility," despite its mutability and the confusion to which this gives rise, as a matter of ontology. If one were to plot their places on a Platonic line of authenticity, Latin would be found to be a mere representation of vernacular speech; and Dante is clearly working with some such notion in mind.

An important element of Dante's position is the remarkable argument that Latin and the vernacular are more or less entirely unrelated. In particular, it follows from the fact that he regards the vernacular as the more ancient language that it cannot be descended from Latin. If anything, the opposite would on Dante's account be true, Latin being a stable form of the vernacular constructed along grammatical principles. It was over a century after Dante's essay before humanist scholars reached a consensus that ancient culture was not bilingual, writing the Latin that survived in classical literature while speaking a vernacular of which no record survived, but that it rather spoke and wrote a plural Latin that, far from being impervious to change, underwent many changes over time and in different places, emerging as the various forms of the vernacular spoken in contemporary Italy, Provence, France, Spain, and Romania.[12] This conclusion anticipated the findings of later comparative philologists, which are the basis of modern historical linguistics. But neither Dante's position nor the terms of the humanist debate have failed to leave their mark on the Latin and vernacular cultures of today.

Relevant to this discussion is the idea that the Latin of classical literature was effectively walled off from other kinds of Latin – from the spoken language, regional dialects, and so on. It is an open question how well most ordinary speakers uneducated in the elite dialect could have understood a public literary performance during the early empire: whether the performer was, in effect, speaking one language and the

---

[12] See, variously, Tavoni (1984) and Mazzocco (1993), especially pp. 189–208 (a vigorous critique of Tavoni).

man in the street a quite different one – almost the situation Dante describes in hypothesizing an ancient spoken vernacular that coexisted with an exclusively literary Latin. Linguists stress that modern Romance descends not from the prestige dialect of the Roman elite, but from "vulgar" Latin of the masses. A member of the former group, wishing to tell a friend that he had bought a horse, would have said "equum emi," whereas his lower-class or less-educated counterpart must be presumed to have said something like "ego habeo comparatum unum caballum." It is thus not unusual to employ Latin in its common modern role as a technical language to coin terms such as *sermo cotidianus* or *sermo plebeius* for what an English speaker would call "everyday speech" and to treat an adjective like *harenosus* ("sandy"), when it occurs in serious poetry, as a "borrowing" from the vulgar tongue almost in the same way as if it were a loanword from Greek or Persian. There is, so far as I know, nothing to suggest that Dante's views on this matter have actually influenced modern scholarship; but it is intriguing that linguistic investigation has produced something not altogether unlike Dante's idea that the Latin we still read was not the language that the Romans actually spoke, the language that did produce the vernacular of Dante's own time. Furthermore, it is difficult not to recognize in Dante, in humanist linguistics, and in the work of modern philologists a common theme – namely, that that Latin we know from the written record is a strange and unusual thing, a language so artificial that it cannot serve the purposes of transient, everyday speech – that it is an artificial language, and not a natural one.

The return of the native

The conflict with respect to nature that we find in Dante is not just a quirk; it is a recurring theme, even a defining characteristic of Latin culture. The conflict appears with great clarity and significance in Cicero's dialogue on *Laws*, where the leading idea is that Roman law – or, for the purposes of the dialogue, human law – is based on natural law. Here the idea of natural law gives rise to a discussion that defines in a surprising way just what constitutes a Roman's fatherland.[13]

---

[13] The main issues of interpretation and source criticism are well covered by Rawson (1973); see further Salmon (1972), Bonjour (1975), 78–86, and Eichenberger (1991).

The dialogue on *Laws*, uniquely, is set at Cicero's ancestral villa in Arpinum; the participants are Cicero himself, his brother Quintus, and their friend Atticus. Near the beginning of book 2, Atticus waxes enthusiastic about the setting: "Nature is supreme in matters that concern spiritual repose and diversion," he says, "just as you were saying before with regard to law and justice." He then launches into a spirited encomium of the villa's natural beauty. Cicero replies that he comes whenever possible, since the place is dear to him for a personal reason as well: because it is his *patria*, his "fatherland." His family has lived here for generations; it is still the seat of their ancestral religion. His father spent almost his whole life in a house that still stands, and the place is full of family memories. He compares his paternal homestead to that of the ancient Sabine, Manius Curius Dentatus, and his desire to return to it to that of Odysseus, who preferred his homecoming to Calypso's offer of immortality (2.3).

It is here that the discussion takes an especially interesting turn. Atticus happily admits his complete empathy with Cicero's nostalgia for Arpinum: he too now loves Arpinum, knowing that it is the birthplace of his friend, just as he loves Athens not so much for its "stately and exquisite works of ancient art" as for the great men who lived there (2.4). Note how Atticus appears to miss the point entirely. The expected reply to Cicero's encomium of his birthplace would be, "Yes, I feel just the same way about my own home town." Instead, Atticus inscribes himself within a triangular erotic relationship: Cicero's love for Arpinum produces in Atticus, who loves Cicero, a similar love for Arpinum. Similar, but different, in that Cicero loves Arpinum "naturally," because it is his birthplace; Atticus' love is predicated on a prior social relationship. His comparison of the love he feels for Arpinum to the love he feels for Athens confirms this point. Atticus actually takes pains to deny that he loves Athens as a center of culture, but rather insists that he loves it because, like Arpinum, it was loved by men he loves. The parallelism that Atticus sees between Cicero and himself is false, because the love that Cicero feels for his birthplace is natural, whereas the love felt by Atticus is an acculturated love, something learned – the kind of attachment that an individual might feel to a place with which he has no natural connection at all.

This position makes Atticus a convincing spokesman for the idea that follows. "What did you really mean by the statement you made a while ago, that this place, by which I understand you to refer to Arpinum, is your fatherland?" The reader might be forgiven for wondering, has Atticus been listening? Arpinum is Cicero's birthplace: what other fatherland could he have? Atticus turns out to be thinking much the same thing, but from a different perspective: "Have you, then, *two* fatherlands? Or is our common fatherland the only one? Perhaps you think that wise old Cato's fatherland was not Rome but Tusculum?" This is of course just what any modern reader would think. Cato was born in Tusculum. He moved to Rome and made his career there, but Tusculum remained his fatherland. Or didn't it?

In what follows, Cicero enunciates the doctrine of the two fatherlands. According to this doctrine Cicero, Cato, and all natives of Italian *municipia* have two fatherlands, one by nature or birth and one by citizenship or law – *unam naturae alteram ciuitatis* – "just as the people of your beloved Attica, before Theseus commanded them all to leave the country and move into the city (or *astu*, as they call it) were at the same time citizens of their own towns and of Attica, so we consider as our fatherland both the place where we were born, and also the city into which we have been adopted." Cicero's comparison is telling. Taking his cue from Atticus' well-known love of Athens, which Atticus himself had just made the vehicle of a similar comparison (and which is the source, after all, of his *cognomen*), Cicero explains the condition of modern Italy by appealing to that of ancient Attica. That is to say, the modern custom is justified not by an appeal to nature, as Cicero's derivation of the legal order from the natural order might suggest, but by a paradigm drawn from another culture. Further, the culture to which Cicero appeals is distant, the particular usage that interests him no longer in force. After Theseus' organization of Attica, everyone became a citizen of Athens alone, and presumably lost any tie to a second fatherland. This is not the usage that Cicero has described as obtaining in modern Italy: "so we consider as our fatherland *both* the place into which we have been born, *and also* the city into which we have been adopted." But Cicero then in a sense validates his previous comparison between Rome and Athens and shows that his conception of "fatherland" is in fact much closer to Atticus' than to ours. "But that fatherland must stand first in our esteem in which the name of republic signifies the common citizenship of us all. For this fatherland it is our duty to die, to give of ourselves entirely, to stake and, as it were, to consecrate everything we have. But the fatherland that begot us is not much less sweet than the one that adopted us. Thus I shall never deny that my fatherland is here, though my other fatherland is greater and includes this one within it" (2.5). Atticus finds these arguments completely convincing and admits as much in what can hardly seem to us other than a jarring paradox: "I think I have been brought around to the view that this town that gave you birth is *also* your fatherland" (3.6).

What is most striking here is the way in which the entire conversation, despite the interlocutors' occasional protests to the contrary, systematically privileges the claims of culture over those of nature. Atticus cannot really understand the natural affection that Cicero feels for his birthplace. Furthermore, Cicero, whose attitude seems much closer to ours, understands Atticus' confusion, and seems almost to acknowledge that the natural affection he feels for Arpinum requires some explanation. But the dichotomy represented here between nature and culture, while clear, is obviously complicated by Cicero's claim throughout the dialogue that the basis of human law and culture lies in nature. This exposition takes place under an ideological assumption that the cultural institution being discussed is grounded in nature, while the specific terms in which the discussion is framed relegate nature to a clearly inferior position *vis à vis* the cultural force of law.

In Cicero the need to contain and redeem nature and turn it to the purposes of culture is reflected in all the interlocutors' praise of the natural beauty that surrounds them. As noted above, book 2 of the *Laws* begins with Atticus expressing his enthusiasm for the setting in which he finds himself. It is easy for a modern reader to share in his enthusiasm; but Atticus is no Thoreau. When he compares the natural beauty of Cicero's villa to the grandiose piles of other rusticating aristocrats, he heaps scorn on their penchant for marble floor tiles, paneled ceilings, and aqueducts built to feed artificial "Niles" and "Euripuses," so called. Having once thought that the entire district of Arpinum was merely an uncultivated wilderness, Atticus is now surprised to find how much he enjoys it, and even expresses wonder that Cicero ever cares to go elsewhere – "when you are not at Rome" (2.2). It would seem that the main fault of those other estates is that they use cultural means to counterfeit nature, whereas at Arpinum nature has been improved by culture. Naturalizing culture, counterfeiting nature by sophisticated technical means, it would seem, is bad; but acculturating nature, turning an unspoiled environment to cultivated ends, is good.

This bias comes out in many details. For instance, when Atticus suggests that the threesome continue their conversation on a small island in the Fibrenus, Cicero heartily approves, but not because he wants to enjoy the natural setting *per se:* rather because it is an excellent venue for various cultural activities – or, as Cicero puts it, "that island is a favorite haunt of mine for meditation, writing, and reading" (2.1) – and thus for conducting a philosophical dialogue on law. Later, when they arrive on the island, Atticus indulges in a brief ecphrasis:

> Ah, here we are on the island! What could be more pleasant? The Fibrenus is split by this beak, as it were, and then, divided equally in two, washes over these sides, flows quickly past, speedily comes back together, and so embraces just enough space for a small wrestling floor. This done, as if its *raison d'être* were to provide us with a place for our discussion, it plunges immediately into the Liris and, as if it were being adopted into a patrician family, loses its less famous name and chills those waters considerably; for I have traveled and never felt a colder stream than this: I could hardly dip my foot into it, as Socrates does in Plato's *Phaedrus.* (2.6)

The ecphrasis in Latin literature is never a simple thing, but it is remarkable that Atticus is unable to manage this brief description of a very small island without employing three distinctly different similes. Merely describing the physical shape of the place does not satisfy him. Instead, he finds it necessary to load the island with a variety of over-determined cultural markers. But this need not surprise us. Students are still taught that among the other remarkable features of the famous first simile in the *Aeneid* is the fact that it illustrates a natural phenomenon, a storm at sea, by employing a vehicle from the cultural realm, namely, a political riot – thus reversing the usual Homeric procedure whereby a warrior fights like a lion, weapons fall like hail, and so forth. Atticus' similes are like Virgil's in this respect. The point of the island that splits Fibrenus' stream he calls a "beak" (*rostrum*). The word does of course mean a bird's beak, but in this aquatic locus it seems rather to denote the metaphorical "beak" or prow of a ship: thus the island, a natural formation, is assimilated to the condition of a boat, a product of human technology – and, it may be worth noting, a potent symbol in primitivist, "golden age" thought of nature violated, of life in an age when humankind could no longer live in deep harmony with the natural world, but chose or was forced to use technology to make its living: to live in a cultural, and not a natural world. At any rate, given the context and the *dramatis personae*, it is difficult to believe that the word *rostrum* does not also look to those famous prows erected in the Roman Forum as monument to a naval victory over the people of Antium in 338 BC. In the context of Atticus' ecphrasis, the meaning of these *rostra* lies not in their historical significance, but in the fact that they had come to be used as the main speaker's platform in the Forum, a place from which Cicero had addressed the public on many occasions, including several on which he proposed new laws to the people. So, in as much as Cicero in the dialogue is about to promulgate an entire law code in the style of those venerable documents of Roman law, the Twelve Tables, perhaps it is appropriate that Atticus should depict this humble island in terms that recall the very center of Roman civic culture.

But he does not stop at this. Soon he describes the way in which the Fibrenus, as if it existed only to create this island, feeds into the much larger Liris and then disappears, just as a man adopted into a patrician family loses the name to which he was born and assumes that of his adoptive father. Again culture illustrates nature, and the parallel contrasts between on the one hand natural and adoptive fatherlands earlier in the discussion (Italian and Roman respectively), and on the other hand natural and adoptive families (plebeian and patrician respectively), can hardly be missed.

Like the Fibrenus feeding the Liris, this simile quickly flows into another. But it is worth turning back to see how the transition soon to take place is anticipated. The very same sentence in which Atticus figures the island as the Roman Forum goes on to call the little plot of ground that rises from the stream a "wrestling floor" or *palaestra* that looks almost as if it were designed to provide the three friends with a place for their discussion. The metaphor by which dialectic is figured as an athletic contest is common, but we should not for that reason overlook its specificity here. In the first place, *palaestra* is a loanword from the Greek. Latin is full of Greek borrowings; but a sentence in which an unnamed place of no special significance, a place so small that it hardly exists except as a setting for the imaginary dialogue that is the only document even suggesting that the place ever did exist – a sentence in which such a place is figured first as the center of Roman culture and then as a *palaestra*, one among many centers of Greek culture, deserves to be taken seriously. And in fact, the same movement from Rome to Greece occurs earlier, when Cicero compares his paternal homestead to that of Dentatus, and his desire to return to it to that of Odysseus.

The same movement from Roman to Greek is repeated within the ecphrasis when Atticus comments on the chill waters of the Fibrenus. First, he says, they are so cold that they cool the larger stream of the Liris, into which they flow and then lose their name, like a man of humble birth who is adopted into a patrician family. Then, he says, they are so cold that he could hardly stand to test them with his foot, as Socrates tests the waters of the Ilissus in the Platonic dialogue *Phaedrus* (230b5–8). Of the many observations that could be made about this remarkable transition, I note only that the shift from patrician (and thus *a fortiori* Roman) to Greek, and to the *Phaedrus* in particular, brings the entire movement of this extraordinary passage to a close: for Cicero has of course been thinking of Plato all along. In a general sense, his entire project of writing philosophical dialogues is inspired by Plato's example; more specifically, his earlier dialogue on *The Republic* and this one on *Laws* are explicitly modeled on the Platonic dialogues of the same names. In particular, the idea that nature is the source of human law is an important theme in Plato's *Laws* (especially in book 10), even if Cicero has other sources in mind as well. And finally, the prominent thematic role allotted to nature in Cicero's proem is inspired by Plato's *Phaedrus*, which informs the entire passage under discussion, as Cicero at last discloses by having Atticus cite as his own model the behavior of the Platonic Socrates in that very dialogue.

In so many of the examples I have discussed in this chapter, the claims of culture are clearly privileged over those of nature. This much should by now be obvious. But the line of interpretation I have been following leads to a further conclusion as inescapable as it is surprising. Time and again, the appeal to nature conceals a much stronger discursive move, a form of self-fashioning that is practiced by one culture – namely, Latin – taking as its model another culture – namely, Greek. Cicero's natural law is a Greek concept that in fact has little to do with the law code that he eventually promulgates. Similarly, the appeal to nature in Latin grammar, along with the very idea of systematic grammar and most of its actual details, is borrowed from the Greeks. And

Aeneas, as Virgil's script of national identity reaches its denouement, finally ceases to be Trojan and begins to become Roman by taking on more exactly than ever the characteristic traits of the greatest Greek cultural paradigm, the hero Achilles. Again and again, when Latin culture confronts itself and inquires into its nature, it sees Greek.

Indeed, these ingredients – a nativist or naturalist impulse, manifested either as the worship of Trojan Aeneas in the guise of Pater Indiges or as praise of a Frankish king for his command of Latin; a coming together through triangular desire, whether in conflict over Lavinia, or in mutual affection for a particular landscape; a scene of initiation, by which the barbarians' acclamation of Titus as father of their second fatherland and Jupiter's capitulation to Juno provide the script for countless iterations played out across the centuries by thousands of readers, students of Latin, students of grammar; these ingredients may be said to define an important strand in the master narrative by which Latin culture continues to write itself.

To conclude, let me draw attention to one further feature shared by Atticus and Cicero, by Aeneas, by the spectators at Titus' games, by Venantius' Frankish patrons, by Dante, and by ourselves. It is worth remembering that someone like Atticus is that rarest of creatures in Latin culture: a native Roman, Roman by birth, or, as the phrase goes, "a Roman of Rome." None of Atticus' own literary works survives. If one were to appear, Cicero's friend would join Julius Caesar in a very select group, doubling the number of native Roman authors whose works still exist; for Atticus, as his biographer Cornelius Nepos tells us, was from a very old Roman family. His confusion in the dialogue I have been discussing is thus the more readily understandable. Atticus did not have two fatherlands, one natural and the other cultural. His only *patria* was Rome.[14] It is therefore at least intelligible that he should be unfamiliar with the idea that many Romans have two fatherlands. But in other respects, Atticus' position remains strange and allows further interesting observations.

First I would note that Atticus does not have the affective relationship for Rome, his natural fatherland, that Cicero has for Arpinum. Rather, he has the very feelings towards Rome that he expects Cicero to

---

[14] For important observations on Rome as a city of aliens and exiles, see Edwards (1996), 15–18, 110–35. On affection for Rome, see Bonjour (1975).

have, and that Cicero insists he does have: feelings of duty, responsibility, and so forth. But in neither case are these really feelings of affection, such as Cicero (and Atticus following Cicero) expresses for Arpinum. But Atticus does have an affective relationship for his adoptive fatherland, Athens. His situation is thus the inverse of Cicero's: a sense of duty rather than affection towards his birthplace, and a sense of affection for adoptive homes deriving from his love for various non-Romans, friends and cultural exemplars, whom he admires.

It is also worth noting that Atticus, a native Roman, requires Cicero, an arriviste, to interpret his own position for him.[15] As a Roman he has no sense of a natural fatherland as distinct from an adoptive one, and he regards his natural fatherland almost as if it were not his birthplace at all. Cicero's position is fraught with complementary ironies: a consular, he was also a new man, reaching the highest annual office in the government but unable to penetrate the inner circle of the ancient aristocracy. He was not a native Roman, but became, if anyone, *the* exemplar of latinity for future generations. As such he is heir to a long line of foreigners who won their places in the pantheon of Latin culture, a group that includes the Greek Livius Andronicus, the Campanian Gnaeus Naevius, the Messapian Quintus Ennius, and many others; and he is the progenitor of an even longer line that includes the Iberians Quintilian and Martial, the Africans Augustine and Apuleius, Britons like Alcuin ... The list could be infinitely extended.

Finally, I would note that there is an interesting ambivalence in Atticus' position, one that is not, however, made explicit in the dialogue. Atticus was a member of an old Roman family, the Pomponii; but the name Pomponius is not Latin. If it were, it would be Quintilius (an older form, Quinctilius, is also attested). Pomponius is a Sabellian form of the same name, rather like such variants as Anderson and Anderssen. Many other ancient Roman families bore Sabellian names as well. Indeed, tradition even records that the first king, Romulus, murdered his twin brother Remus rather than suffer diminution of his kingly prerogative, and yet accepted as coregent for a time the Sabellian Titus Tatius. The biological twin is removed only to be replaced by a cultural one who is, moreover, foreign. So Sabellian and Latin culture existed side by side in archaic Rome, as Germanic and Latin culture did

---

[15] On the related issue of Cicero's position as a *nouus homo* see Bonjour (1975), 79.

in medieval Francia, and became in many ways indistinguishable. Officially the oldest Latin family in Rome was that of the Julii; but to claim this distinction even the Julii, with several other families, had to claim Trojan ancestry. The point is, there are no native Romans, no national myth of an autochthonous people. All members of Latin culture must journey to Rome, each in his or her own way; we modern Latins are in this respect no different from any other member of our culture at any time, in any place.

CHAPTER

2

The poverty of our ancestral speech

Poor relations

Again and again, when Latin culture confronts itself and inquires into its nature, it sees Greek. The conclusion that often follows is that Latin is derivative and inferior – that in trying to be Greek Latin dooms itself to epigonal status. For the Latin speaker an authentic and unmediated connection between nature and culture is unattainable. But such a relationship is imagined to exist for Greek, and this belief becomes a source of envy, perceived inferiority, and self-deprecation. To the Greek language Latin culture ascribes not only a more fundamental authenticity, but other qualities as well – a capacity for beautiful and subtle expression, for instance – that it feels unable to claim for itself. In various ways some such view of the relationship between Latin and Greek has been common throughout history. Its validity is apparently supported by the facts of linguistic development, by the literary history of the two languages, and by the explicit testimony of Latin authors themselves. But what has been commonly felt or is apparently true should not blind us to other important ways of construing this relationship and of defining Latin culture.[1]

The theme under discussion runs through Latin literature and through the reception of Latin literature in all periods. So common a theme deserves a name: call it "the poverty topos." It occurs in several different guises. Most obviously, poverty connotes deficient semantic power. This idea was given definitive expression by Lucretius, who

---

[1] On this problem see Feeney (1998), passim, especially 6–11, 47–67, 74–75.

mentions several times the challenge involved in composing a poem on Greek philosophy when faced with the impoverished resources of the Latin language (*DRN* 1.136–39, 830–33; 3.258–61). A second aspect of poverty has to do with an inability to express things beautifully. "Greek," according to Isidore of Seville, "is considered an especially splendid language among the rest of the nations; for it is more resonant than Latin and all other languages" (*Orig.* 9.1). Very frequently these two kinds of poverty are linked to one another and to a third kind, a lack of real competence in Greek: "Latins," according to the fourth-century "Ambrosiaster," "have the habit of singing in Greek, enjoying the sound of the words but without knowing what they say." And ignorance inevitably breeds a fourth kind of poverty, a perception of lack that leads directly to aspiration or desire for what is ultimately unattainable on *a fortiori* grounds. An anecdote from St. Gall sums up a commonly expressed medieval perspective on the two cultures.[2] When a young man who desired to learn Greek declared himself to the Duchess Hadwig, who he hoped might teach him, he expressed his wish in the following passable hexameter:

Esse uelim Grecus, cum sim uix, domna, Latinus.

Though scarcely Latin, mistress, I would like to be Greek.

This self-deprecating request conforms to a well-established hierarchy between the two languages, one that is most famously reflected, perhaps, in Ben Jonson's comment on Shakespeare's "small Latine and lesse Greeke," though the element of desire in the young man's epigram deserves special notice. Fifth, desire for Greek is linked to the motifs of rarity and cost, often figured in comparisons with costly artifacts and by emphasis on the sheer difficulty (the cost as measured in time and energy) involved in learning the language, as in the often-cited remark of Samuel Johnson: "Greek, sir, is like lace: every man gets as much of it as he can." For our immediate purposes, it is important to remember that the author of this last saying was counted one of the chief Latin scholars of his day, which raises the final point: an exalted valuation of unattainable Greek learning occasionally gives rise, as we shall see, to contempt for Latin, the indigent language, the language of paupers.

---

[2] Ekkehard, *Casus S. Galli* 94, ed. Haefele (1980), 194.

These different aspects of the poverty topos appear in various combinations throughout Latin culture from antiquity to the present day. The fact that they do appear in antiquity may be taken to ratify the attitudes that they embody: that if the ancient Romans regarded their language as impoverished with respect to Greek, then there must be something to the idea. But it is often the case that what look like simple and unambiguous statements mean something quite other than what they appear to say. In this particular case, as we shall see, "poverty" is not identical with "inferiority."

The Greeks had a word for it

To gain some purchase on the idea of linguistic poverty, let us consider Valerius Maximus on stratagems.[3] Throughout ten books of *Memorable Deeds and Sayings* containing almost a thousand chapter headings, only this one (7.4) happens to be in Greek. It is in Greek, the author informs us, because the chapter concerns a subject for which Latin has no word: "That aspect of cleverness which is distinguished and remote from any reproof, whose works, since they cannot be properly expressed in ⟨our own⟩ manner of speaking, are called by the Greek term 'stratagems'."[4] This is quite an ostentatious way of announcing a subject. Is it not also just a bit disingenuous? In the ensuing series of tales illustrating the concept of "stratagems," Valerius uses the following Latin synonyms: *astutia, calliditas, consilium,*[5] *dissimulatio, dolus, fallacia, insidiae,* and *prudentia.* The impression created by this display is hardly one of meager resources. Perhaps it is true that Latin has no single, comprehensive term that embraces all of the above. The possibility also exists, however, that Valerius simply did not want to use a Latin word that might adequately render the idea because he preferred to name trickery with a foreign word in order to mark such behavior as un-Roman.

[3] On Valerius in general see Bloomer (1992); on *strategemata* and grecisms see pp. 27, 238. On the Greek and Latin terminology for stratagems, see Wheeler (1988).

[4] *Illa uero pars calliditatis egregia et ab omni reprehensione procul remota, cuius opera, quia appellatione ⟨nostra⟩ uix apte exprimi possunt, Graeca pronuntiatione "strategemata" dicuntur* (7.4).

[5] Not without appropriate qualification, as in *perquam callido genere consilii, ut uafro ita periculoso consilio,* and *sagacibus consiliis.*

The *exempla* that follow bear this assumption out. One concerns Tarquinius Superbus and his son Sextus, partners in deceiving the people of Gabii. This famous episode shortly preceded the treacherous king's expulsion, freedom from foreign rule, and the establishment of the Republic. Several other cases involve the use of stratagems against perfidious foreigners. King Tullus Hostilius uses deception against the legendarily faithless Alban leader Mettius Fufetius; a ruse saves the Capitol during the Gallic invasion; and Quintus Metellus outfoxes the Celtiberians. Finally, three exempla involve the Carthaginians, throughout Latin culture the very type of the treacherous foe. The consuls Claudius Nero and Livius Salinator get the better of the Carthaginian general Hasdrubal; Agathocles of Syracuse raises a Carthaginian siege by attacking Carthage itself; and at Cannae the Romans succumb to the superior craftiness of that master of perfidy, the greatest villain in Roman history, Hannibal. Hannibal, it is true, appears frequently in Valerius' work, so his inclusion here is not in itself especially noteworthy. Nevertheless, he concludes a list of stratagems, which had been defined at the beginning of this chapter as "that aspect of cleverness which is distinguished and remote from any reproof," but which are ultimately denounced by the author in a fit of indignation with the words, "This is what Punic bravery was, a thing fortified with trickery, sabotage, and deception. And that is our most irrefutable excuse for how our own valor was got around, since we were deceived rather than conquered."[6]

The greatly diminished honor of the stratagem at the end of the chapter is in effect predicted by Valerius' selection and flaunting of a foreign word – which itself proves to be a kind of stratagem – to designate the concept in his title. The stratagem is something for which Latin has no word because (Valerius suggests) it is an inherently un-Roman concept, something to which Romans resort under the yoke of foreign kings or in response to the treachery of an alien foe. The pervasive association in Latin culture between Greek ethnicity and a penchant for trickery supports this interpretation. And Valerius' ploy is no isolated

---

[6] *Haec fuit Punica fortitudo, dolis et insidiis et fallacia instructa; quae nunc certissima circumuentae uirtutis nostrae excusatio est, quoniam decepti magis quam uicti sumus* (4 ext. 2).

example; rather it is an instance of what looks like a rhetorical commonplace. Quintilian cites with approval the elder Cato's commentary on the word *nothus:*

> The Greeks call a person of illegitimate birth *nothus.* We have no Latin word for this phenomenon, as Cato testifies in one of his orations, and so we use the foreign term.[7]

Cato, Valerius, and Quintilian are clearly playing on the idea that the resources of Latin are more restricted than those of Greek. The idea was evidently a commonplace, probably even in Cato's day. But this commonplace figures Latin culture as morally superior because the Latin language lacks words for certain shameful ideas, and so must borrow from Greek, the linguistic richness of which is a symptom of moral depravity.[8] Poverty, yes; inferiority, no.

On almost knowing Greek

For Matthew Arnold, "The power of the Latin classic is in character, that of the Greek is in beauty. Now character is capable of being taught, learnt, and assimilated; beauty hardly." This conception would seem to be at odds with the notion of Greek culture's universality (cf. Shelley's "We are all Greeks"). Certainly Arnold implies that Latin character is in principle capable of being acquired by all, and thus may be regarded as possessing a potential for universality. But alongside this liberal view stands another, much more conservative and indeed aristocratic one. Appreciation of Greek beauty is universal not in the sense that all of us may acquire it; for, according to Arnold, none of us may acquire it. But some of us evidently are born with it and therefore make up a kind of natural aristocracy of culture. There is, it seems, no telling in whom this capacity will occur, or why. One may labor to acquire the character that comes with Latin culture but in doing so, one must not make the mistake of presuming that an affinity for Greek beauty will come with it. If anything, the opposite may be the case.

---

[7] *Nothum qui non sit legitimus Graeci uocant, Latinum rei nomen, ut Cato quoque in oratione quadam testatus est, non habemus, ideoque utimur peregrino* (*IO* 3.6.97 = fr. 239 Malcovati (1976), 1.95).

[8] Cf. Adams (1982), 228–30.

These sentiments of Arnold's may seem quaintly Victorian, but in fact they form an important part of a continuum in intellectual history that has consistently preferred Greek to Latin studies, finding in the former a richer repository of human values. Thomas Habinek has traced this preference from its inception in the work of the German Romantics to its institutionalization in the American academy through the influence of B. L. Gildersleeve.[9] Outside the academy, the preference for Greek over Latin is even more pronounced. In this respect, the modernist esthetic movement was entirely typical. One of its more notable characteristics is the extremely high value that it placed on Greek – not just on Greek literature, which had been in the ascendant since the Romantic period, but on the language itself, which came to be valued as a medium ideally suited to the principles that modernist art held dear.

Virginia Woolf is one of the founding heroines of modernist thought. She was also obsessed with Greek – the Greek language, the study of Greek, and Greek scholars.[10] Latin culture she took more or less for granted, and when she did make use of it in her fiction, the result would be a speech like the one given in *The Waves* to the character Neville as he arrives for the first time at his new school:

> A noble Roman air hangs over these austere quadrangles. Already the lights are lit in the form rooms. Those are laboratories perhaps; and that a library, where I shall explore the exactitude of the Latin language, and step firmly upon the well-laid sentences, and pronounce the explicit, the sonorous hexameters of Virgil; of Lucretius; and chant with a passion that is never obscure or formless the loves of Catullus, reading from a big book, a quarto with margins. I shall lie, too, in the fields among the tickling grasses. I shall lie with my friends under towering elm trees.

Contrast Neville's love of the library and the marginal place he concedes to *plein-air* pastimes with Woolf's own reveries about Athenian drama in the celebrated essay "On Not Knowing Greek":

> That is the quality that first strikes us in Greek literature, the lightning-quick, sneering, out-of-doors manner ... They were speak-

---

[9] Habinek (1998).
[10] On Woolf's idealization of Greek, see Poole (1995), 173–84.

ing to an enormous audience rayed around them on one of those brilliant southern days when the sun was so hot and yet the air so exciting. The poet, therefore, had to bethink him, not of some theme which could be read for hours by people in privacy, but of something emphatic, familiar, brief, that would carry, instantly and directly, to an audience of seventeen thousand people perhaps, with ears and eyes eager and attentive, with bodies whose muscles would grow stiff if they sat too long without diversion.

Woolf's attitude towards Greek was worshipful. Indeed, she shows a pronounced tendency to idealize the Greek language itself in a number of telling ways, most explicitly perhaps in an early essay entitled "The Perfect Language," an essay that tells us much about her own esthetic ideals. It concludes: "And such is the power of the Greek language that to know even a little of it is to know that there is nothing more beautiful in the world."[11]

Woolf's fantasies about Greek are utterly typical of the modernist sensibility, to which the business of "knowing even a little" is crucial. The point is to want to know Greek while maintaining one's not-quite-perfect ignorance of the language along with one's innocence of what mastering it actually entails. Indeed, in "The Perfect Language" Woolf actually states that people who know Greek well are not only extremely talented and rare ("the few who read Sophocles perfectly," as she amazingly puts it, "are about as singular as acrobats flying through space from bar to bar") but, by overcoming the difficulty in reading it, they have lost sight of its full value. Familiarity breeds contempt. There is a notion that the unfamiliar territory that is the Greek language resembles other artifacts, like Dogon masks, admired by the moderns for their directness, simplicity, and clarity, for the insight that they give us, despite or because of their strangeness, into our essential, irreducible humanity. The attitude in question here is not unrelated to that of Shelley; but the crucial difference between this Romantic trope and modernist ideology is that while Greek language and culture had once been valued as the civilizing force that raised us out of our superstitious

---

[11] Even those who share this opinion may be amused to learn that Woolf penned this rhapsody in an enthusiastic review of W. R. Paton's Loeb edition of the Greek Anthology (1917).

torpor and into the light of reason, in our own era Greek has been perceived as a language informed by cultural authenticity but relatively unencumbered by civilization's discontents.

The language of civilization, of course, and of people like Neville, is Latin, which was much more familiar than Greek to people of Woolf's generation, a language forced on schoolchildren as a civilizing agent rather than a rare artifact to be savored by one possessed of a mature esthetic sensibility. An unfortunate aspect of the modernist delight in Greek was therefore a countervailing contempt for Latin. The difference between the perceived value of education in the two languages is reflected clearly in the prejudices of W. B. Yeats as expressed in a fanciful letter to his son's schoolmaster:

> Dear Sir,
> My son is now between nine and ten and should begin Greek at once and be taught by the Berlitz method that he may read as soon as possible that most exciting of all stories, the Odyssey, from that landing in Ithaca to the end. Grammar should come when the need comes. As he grows older he will read to me the great lyric poets and I will talk to him about Plato. Do not teach him one word of Latin. The Roman people were the classic decadence, their literature form without matter. They destroyed Milton, the French seventeenth and our own eighteenth century, and our schoolmasters even to-day read Greek with Latin eyes. Greece, could we but approach it with eyes as young as its own, might renew our youth. Teach him mathematics as thoroughly as his capacity permits. I know that Bertrand Russell must, seeing that he is such a featherhead, be wrong about everything, but as I have no mathematics I cannot prove it. I do not want my son to be as helpless ... If you teach him Greek and mathematics and do not let him forget the French and German that he already knows you will do for him all that one man can do for another. If he wants to learn Irish after he is well founded in Greek, let him – it will clear his eyes of the Latin miasma.[12]

This letter was never sent and can hardly be regarded as entirely serious. But Yeats, in addition to being the finest lyric poet of the last century at least, was also a famous crank – a man, after all, who had monkey tes-

[12] Yeats (1962), 320–21.

ticles surgically implanted into his own body in order to enhance his virility – and his eccentric opinions about all sorts of topics are well documented. In respect of Latin and Greek, however, it is really his colorful manner of expression that is eccentric, not the opinion itself. He despises Latin, but praises Greek in terms that recall the banal rhapsodies that had been standard since the late eighteenth century and in fact surpasses them in the fatuous suggestion that a ten-year-old boy might be taught to read Homer without compromising his innocence of grammar. But his position is not so very different from Woolf's when she says that to appreciate Greek fully, "one would have, no doubt, to be born a Greek." It would be essential that one's experience of the language come to perfection naturally and without conscious effort or deliberate study.

Mapping the linguistic domain

Grammar is depicted by Yeats as a Latin vice. Lord, what would he say, did he realize that traditional Latin grammar is cribbed almost entirely from Greek? If he had known anything about the ancient grammarians, of course, Yeats probably would have interpreted what he knew as more evidence of Latin decadence; and the Latin appropriation of Greek grammar is indeed a remarkable phenomenon. It is linked, obviously enough, to the motif of territorial conquest; but this motif relates to the poverty topos in surprising ways.

If in antiquity a speaker of Greek made a mistake in usage, that was called a "solecism" (σολοικισμός). If the mistake was instead one of grammar or syntax, it was called a "barbarism" (βαρβαρισμός). These types of error can be, almost literally, plotted on a linguistic map of the Mediterranean basin. To commit a solecism places the offender, amusingly, in the Greek city of Soli. Located in ancient Cilicia on the southern coast of modern Turkey, Soli was home to such cultural luminaries as the philosopher Chrysippus and the poets Philemon and Aratus; but it was also notorious for the linguistic faults that produced the grammatical concept of solecism. To commit a barbarism, however, was evidently a graver offence. Such a mistake placed a Greek speaker in the company of those who dwelled beyond the pale of the Hellenic world, which is to say, in the region where Greek was not spoken. Nor is the linguistic map defined by these terms alone. In fact, the very concept of correct speech is culturally and even ethnically defined. When a Greek grammarian speaks of linguistic correctness, he speaks not merely of "rightness" (ὀρθότης), but of "Greekness" itself (ἑλληνισμός). Thus solecism and barbarism are described as if they were offences not merely against the rules of grammar, but against cultural and ethnic identity as well.

From a Greek perspective, a speaker of Latin should be a βάρβαρος; and occasionally a Latin speaker actually incurs this charge. But Latin grammar is basically Greek grammar translated and adapted as necessary. This situation produced a certain amount of strain. One particularly ironic area of tension is the matter of correct usage that we have been discussing. Correctness in Latin was called, not *rectitudo* or *proprietas*, but *latinitas*. Behind this concept stands the ἑλληνισμός of the Greeks. It would not do for Roman grammarians merely to borrow the term as *hellenismus*; rather, they invented an analogical ideal, based on the Greek, but reflecting a linguistic difference. This is a wholly understandable move. But in adapting Greek linguistic concepts to Roman realities, the grammarians went only so far. If a Latin speaker made a mistake in formal grammar or syntax, it was called a *barbarismus*, just as in Greek; and by the very same token, but even more bizarrely, a mistake in usage was called, precisely, a *soloecismus*. There is in a sense nothing unusual in this: the terms are simply borrowed from the Greek grammarians, and they may be no more remarkable than when an American speaks of "the King's English." And yet they are remarkable, for while the King of England once claimed sovereignty over much of the Americas, the Romans were never situated within the linguistic realm of ἑλληνισμός. The Greek concept of barbarism originally included the Romans, whose Latin language was a barbarian form of speech. The Romans borrowed this concept and applied it, more selectively than the Greeks, to foreign peoples.

This grammatical geography is directly implicated in the poverty topos. Cicero, in a certain mood, could invert the topos completely. At one point he boasts that in writing philosophy "we seem to have made such progress that the Greeks do not surpass us even in vocabulary" (*De natura deorum* 1.8); and again, more generally, "I have often observed that Latin is not only not destitute (*inopem*), as is vulgarly believed, but that it is even richer (*locupletiorem*) than Greek" (*De finibus* 1.10). The etymology of *locuples* refers to the extensive land holdings in which honest Roman wealth traditionally consisted. It is tempting to see an implied connection here (as of course there was in fact) with the enormous personal estates acquired by the Roman elite and the vast expansion of public holdings in the form of provinces – including, of course, Greece. But for another purpose, Cicero would deploy the motif more conventionally by linking territorial to linguistic poverty: "Greek is read among practically all peoples; Latin is contained within its own borders, and those quite small" (*pro Archia* 23).

Such passages show that Latin culture clearly envied Greece its linguistic empire and was anxious about its own place on the map. The varying perspectives adopted by Cicero indicate once again that this anxiety was multivalent, or at least bipolar. Latin is either a wealthy landowner or not, either a linguistic colony of Greece or not, but desirous, always, of occupying Greek linguistic holdings not as a usurper, but as a rightful owner who might legitimately relegate offenders against *latinitas* – which is to say, against ἑλληνισμός – to Soli or exile them to barbary.

The most extreme manifestation of the tendency to assimilate Latin to Greek consists in the belief that two languages are in fact the same or, more precisely, that Latin is actually a dialect of Greek. It is not clear that many Romans or Greeks subscribed to or indeed cared very much one way or the other about this theory or the issues that it raises for us. But although the idea was probably never very widespread, it is definitely attested and deserves more recognition and consideration than it commonly receives. The general idea is that Latin was a dialect of West Greece, probably a branch of Aeolic, and that old Latin inscriptions revealed the common identity of the two languages. Our main witness is Dionysius of Halicarnassus, who also thought (following earlier writers) that Odysseus was, along with Aeneas, co-founder of Rome.[13] When approached unreflectively, evidence like this looks like yet another symptom of an intense desire on the part of Latin culture to be Greek, to make any and every case on behalf of its Greekness – to gain an owner's stake in at least the linguistic wealth of Greece. What better explanation for Latin acquiescence in the face of Greek cultural hegemony than to discover that Latin not only desires to be Greek, but

[13] Solmsen (1986).

actually is Greek? But it is in truth more likely that such theories arose from quite the opposite direction. Certainly the ancient Romans, however much they may have prided themselves on acquiring a measure of Greek culture, never stopped insisting on the difference between the Greeks and themselves. It is possible that Dionysius was writing with a view to flattering his cultivated Roman patrons by suggesting that, deep down, they were as Greek as he was. On the other hand, it seems more likely that Dionysius was writing primarily for a Greek audience and that part of his purpose was to reassure his readers that this upstart culture that had taken permanent control of Greek affairs, that these foreign rulers were not really barbarians (as Demosthenes had considered Philip), but Greeks more or less like themselves.[14] If this is the case, then the theory that would make Latin a dialect of Greek is the other side of the poverty topos, a reflex of Greek hope that the linguistic domain of ἑλληνισμός had not passed into foreign hands after all.

The language of reality

Can Latin be adequately represented as a poor relation of Greek? I hope it is clear that the situation was much more complicated than that. Nevertheless, the poverty topos circulated widely, and someone must have believed in it. It was Lucretius, as I observed earlier, who stated the problem most succinctly and memorably:

> Nec me animi fallit Graiorum obscura reperta
> difficile inlustrare Latinis uersibus esse,
> multa nouis uerbis praesertim cum sit agendum
> propter egestatem linguae et rerum nouitatem ...

> Nor does it escape me how difficult it is to cast light in Latin verses upon the obscure discoveries of the Greeks, especially when having to treat of many points by means of unfamiliar words, thanks to the poverty of the language and the novelty of the material ...

> *DRN* 1.136–39

In two later passages (1.832, 3.260) Lucretius recurs to this idea, each time citing "the poverty of our ancestral speech" as a factor that

---

[14] Gabba (1991).

inhibits him in his chosen task. The expression he uses, *patrii sermonis egestas*, crystalizes the general idea announced earlier in a way that has conditioned the manner in which we have thought about Latin ever since. Latin is impoverished compared to Greek in ways that the modern linguist can measure with great accuracy. Compared to Latin, Greek has an extra voice, number, mood, and tense; more than twice as many participles; a definite article; a wealth of minor adverbs or "particles"; and a vastly larger vocabulary, including the many compounds that Greek forms much more readily and in greater profusion than Latin. Latin has one extra case, but Greek is much more various in using its oblique cases to express different ideas. Greek also possesses several dialects, many of which contributed to literary culture in distinctive ways, while correct latinity is measured by the standards established by a few generations of the ruling class of a single city. This list of differences is hardly complete, but it gives some idea of the specific formal resources that the Greek speaker had at his or her disposal but that the Latin speaker lacked. It is partly the existence of these resources that explains the superiority of Greek to Latin in all manner of expression, from the intellectual subtlety of philosophical dialectic to the emotional and psychological range of poetry and historiography. How could the Latin speaker schooled in Greek not feel that the *patrius sermo* is somehow indequate?

In certain areas the perception of inadequacy becomes acute. It is the beauty of Greek (Arnold, Woolf) that accounts in large part for its reputation as a poetic language; and the Greeks, according to received wisdom, invented philosophy, both the word and the idea. The Romans followed the Greeks in both fields, often at quite a distance, and their inferiority is often referred to the narrower resources of Latin speech. No wonder Lucretius, who aspired to write a philosophical treatise in poetic form, was moved to comment on the constraints imposed upon him by the limited capacity of his native tongue to embody these two forms of discourse independently, let alone in combination.

Modern readers, even the most critical, want to believe their ancient authors. But they are not always trustworthy, and Latin poets in particular are an extremely duplicitous lot. Lucretius bruits clarity as one of his chief ideals, and in fact he usually is clear; but his love of clarity does not prevent him from writing so as to create depths of meaning that may not be instantly apparent, or from indulging in a degree of irony. It is unlikely that he was the first to compare Latin and Greek to the disadvantage of the *patrius sermo*. Is it possible that he introduces the idea playfully, perhaps even to establish the superiority of Latin over Greek as a medium of philosophical expression?[15] Let us return to his actual words:

Nec me animi fallit Graiorum obscura reperta
difficile inlustrare Latinis uersibus esse,
multa nouis uerbis praesertim cum sit agendum
propter egestatem linguae et rerum nouitatem.
Sed tua me uirtus tamen et sperata uoluptas
suauis amicitiae quemuis efferre laborem
suadet et inducit noctes uigilare serenas
quaerentem dictis quibus et quo carmine demum
clara tuae possim praepandere lumina menti,
res quibus occultas penitus conuisere possis.

Nor does it escape me how difficult it is to cast light in Latin verses upon the obscure discoveries of the Greeks, especially when having to treat of many points by means of unfamiliar words, thanks to the poverty of the language and the novelty of the material. But your character and the pleasure of sweet friendship that I long for persuade me to bear any difficulty and induce me to stay watchful through the clear nights looking for just the right language and poetry with which I might open to your mind the clear light by which you may see deeply into hidden matters.

1.136–45

The language of this passage encourages the view that Lucretius' contrast between light and dark is not a simple matter of throwing a switch. He hopes to be able to "open the clear lights" to Memmius' mind. What does this mean, exactly? To shine lights onto Memmius' mind? To reveal lights to his mind? To open the lights of his mind? Are these lights, as often in Latin, eyes, which Lucretius wants to "open for the first time" (*praepandere*)? And what of the "things deeply hidden?" Will

---

[15] On this issue see Sedley (1998), 35–61.

they be apparent as soon as Lucretius "opens the lights to/for/of
[Memmius'] mind," or will Memmius catch sight of them only gradually, through effort and repeated attempts? The poet's own active quest
for the right words, which come to him only gradually, through effort
and over time (and by dark of night at that) may suggest what his
reader's experience will be as well. In fact, it is notable that Lucretius
sets up an entire array of strong contrasts as the movement from error
to truth parallels those from darkness to light, obscurity to clarity, prose
(at least by implication) to poetry – and, not least, from Greek to Latin.

It is intriguing to find Latin, the impoverished language, on the side
of light, clarity, and truth while Greek lines up on the side of darkness,
obscurity, and error. Of course the correlation can simply be explained
away. Memmius and Lucretius are Latin speakers. Lucretius seizes the
privileged position of the linguistic and cultural interpreter who can
make clear to practical Roman Memmius (who stands for a much
wider, practical-minded Roman audience) a world that is theoretical
and Greek. But this explanation rings false. It is difficult to assess the
role of Memmius with precision, but to the best of our knowledge
Lucretius is addressing a man who actually owned a site in Athens that
had once contained Epicurus' house. It seems unlikely that such a man
should need elementary instruction in philosophy or the services of an
interpreter of Greek. Perhaps the relationship that Lucretius imagines
here between Latin and Greek is one of those truths that lurks far
beneath the surface of things and reveals itself only with time to those
who make enough effort? However that may be, Lucretius repeats the
pattern we have noticed in a way that leaves no doubt about what he
means. The two subsequent passages in which the poverty motif occurs
were obviously composed as an artfully related pair:

> Nunc et Anaxagorae scrutemur homoeomerian
> quam Grai memorant nec nostra dicere lingua
> concedit nobis **patrii sermonis egestas,**
> sed tamen ipsam rem facile est exponere uerbis.

> And now let us scrutinize what the Greeks call Anaxagoras' ὁμοιο-
> μέρεια, which **the poverty of our ancestral speech** does not permit us
> to say in our our own language, though the thing itself is easy to
> explain in words. 1.830–33

Nunc ea quo pacto inter sese mixta quibusque
compta modis uigeant rationem reddere auentem
abstrahit inuitum **patrii sermonis egestas;**
sed tamen, ut potero summatim attingere, tangam.

Now though eager to render an account of how and in what ways
these things, mixed together and compacted, flourish, **the poverty of
our ancestral speech** draws me away against my will; but to the extent
that I can treat of the subject in summary fashion, I shall.

3.258–61

In the not very distant past it was usual to regard such Lucretian
doublets as signs of his poem's unfinished state. It is difficult nowadays
to understand this reaction; parallelisms of this kind do not just happen.
Of course, it is possible to regard repetition as a symptom of "poverty,"
whether in language, poetic inspiration, or both, and Lucretius is a
very repetitive poet. Perhaps he was aware that his repetitions might be
taken as indicating the poverty of both the Latin language and his own
powers of invention, but challenged readers to see these faults as
advantages by showing them how well a severely restricted style might
serve his message.

The passage from book I on presocratic doxography illustrates this
point admirably.[16] In this extremely one-sided review, Heraclitus,
Empedocles, and Anaxagoras are represented not only by characteristic
philosophical ideas, but by their linguistic characters as well; and this
dwelling on language becomes an important element of Lucretius' self-
fashioning.

One obvious feature of the doxography is that Heraclitus and Anaxagoras are openly mocked, while Empedocles receives a measure of
respect, honor, and even affection. Indeed, we are told that Sicily produced nothing more brilliant (*nil praeclarius* 729), nothing more holy or
wondrous or even more dear (*nec sanctum magis et mirum carumque*

---

[16] Note that Lucretius' invocation of the "poverty topos" at 3.258–61 follows his
discussion of the four parts of the soul, wind (*aura*), heat (*calor/vapor*), air (*aër*),
and a fourth element that has no name in any language (*east omnino nominis ex-
pers* 3.242). For this and a number of additional penetrating observations on this
section I am indebted to Denis Feeney (*per litteras*, July 16, 1997). On Lucretius'
presocratic doxography, see Tatum (1984).

730) than this man. Lucretius' respect for Empedocles and disdain for Heraclitus and Anaxagoras is expressed not merely in such terms as these but through geography and language as well. Only Empedocles is designated by his *ethnikon* "Acragantinus" (716) in a passage that implicitly accounts for the philosopher's four-element theory with reference to the physical geography of Sicily:

> Quorum Acragantinus cum primis Empedocles est,
> insula quem triquetris *terrarum* gessit in oris,
> quam fluitans circum magnis anfractibus aequor
> Ionium glaucis aspergit uirus ab *undis*,
> angustoque fretu rapidum mare diuidit undis
> Italiae terrarum oras a finibus eius.
> Hic est uasta Charybdis et hic Aetnaea minantur
> murmura flammarum rursum se colligere iras,
> faucibus eruptos iterum uis ut uomat *ignis*
> ad *caelum*que ferat flammai fulgura rursum.

> Foremost among these is Empedocles of Acragas, whom the three-cornered island brought within the shores of the *earth*, around which flows the Ionian sea that sprinkles it with spray from its grey *waters* and by a narrow passage the voracious sea divides from its borders the shores of the Italian lands. Here is devastating Charybdis, here do Aetna's murmurings of flame threaten to gather back their wrath, that their force might again spew forth *fire* from its jaws and bear the flashing flames back up to the *sky*. 1.716–25

Acragas thus stands for Sicily as a whole, and the island itself is presented as if it were composed of Empedocles' four elements. But the map on which Lucretius situates the Greek poet bears cultural as well as physical features. Indeed, it distorts the facts of physical geography by subordinating them to a rather tendentious cultural argument. For instance, it places Empedocles' homeland very close to that of Lucretius: the same sea-mist that moistens the Sicilian coast rises from the narrow strait that divides the island from the Italian peninsula. This detail obscures the fact that Acragas lies on the western coast of the island about as far from Italy as any Sicilian city can possibly be, and thus establishes a proximity between Empedocles and the Roman world, a proximity that Heraclitus and Anaxagoras totally lack. Indeed, the physical and symbolic distance of these sages from Empedocles (and thus from his neighbor Lucretius) is signaled by another detail in this passage. The Ionian sea (*aequor | Ionium* 718–19) properly lies off the western coast of Greece. It is not unusual to identify it with the water that flows through the Straits of Messina, but to do so in this context may have additional point. Ionia is the home of both Heraclitus of Ephesus and Anaxagoras of Clazomenae. It therefore seems possible to interpret Lucretius' geographical reference as a metonymic symbol: just as a narrow strait of the "Ionian" Sea is all that separates Sicily from Italy geographically, so is it only those assumptions that Empedocles shares with Ionian philosophers that separate him from Lucretius conceptually.[17]

To accept this interpretation even in part involves an extreme privileging of language over other elemental systems of meaning, and of Lucretius' Latin as the most potent system of all. Consider again Lucretius' claim that Sicily produced nothing more "dear" (*carum* 730) than Empedocles. This statement seems oddly affective until we recall that Lucretius' *cognomen* was Carus, "Dear." It has thus been inferred that the compliment implies a strong affinity between the two poets in Lucretius' mind – that Lucretius means to imply that Empedocles is rather specifically like Lucretius himself.[18] I would add that this connection is established specifically in the Latin language and involves a specifically Roman *cognomen*. Lucretius could not pretend that Empedocles' philosophy did not differ from his own or that Empedocles actually lived in Italy or wrote in Latin, but he could and did use a thematic treatment of Empedocles' theory of four elements, an imaginative approach to Mediterranean geography, and the unique resources of Latin to suggest how highly he valued the Sicilian poet as a forerunner. And this procedure reflects on Lucretius' treatment of Heraclitus and Anaxagoras as well.

In representing Heraclitus as a near-barbarian in his inability to communicate, Lucretius uses the resources of Latin to expose Heraclitus'

---

[17] In a similar vein, Denis Feeney points out to me how Lucretius' language graphically represents the tiny distance between Sicily and Italy: in line 721 a mere preposition separates "the coasts of Italy's lands *from* its [i.e. Sicily's] borders"; and in Latin this mere preposition consists of a single letter (*Italiae terrarum oras **a** finibus eius*) – the first, in fact, of Lucretius' *elementa.*

[18] Kollmann (1971), 89 n. 46.

faults through a series of bilingual puns. Heraclitus, says Lucretius, is first among those who believe that all things are composed of fire, and he is "famous on account of his obscure style":

> Heraclitus init quorum dux proelia primus,
> clarus ob obscuram linguam magis inter inanis
> quamde grauis inter Graios qui uera requirunt.
> Omnia enim stolidi magis admirantur amantque,
> inuersis quae sub uerbis latitantia cernunt,
> ueraque constituunt quae belle tangere possunt
> auris et lepido quae sunt fucata sonore.

> Heraclitus enters the fray as the foremost leader of this group, famous for his obscure language among the vain rather than the serious Greeks who seek the truth. For the foolish admire and love the more all that they see lurking beneath a jumble of words and call true what caresses the ear, tinged with charming sound.   1.638–44

In Latin the specific terms of this argument are formulated in ways that recapitulate the elements of Lucretius' own task, to shed clear light on the obscure discoveries of the Greeks. It seems quite likely that Heraclitus was chosen to lead off this presocratic review for precisely this reason as well as for the poetic possibilities that his name affords. Lucretius calls Heraclitus "famous for his obscure language" (*clarus ob obscuram linguam* 639). This shaft surely contains a pun on the second element of the philosopher's name (i.e. -clitus < κλειτός, "famed" or *clarus* in Latin).[19] The following lines raise the possibility that the rest of the philosopher's name is involved as well.

Heraclitus' fame exists not among the truly wise, but among dolts (*stolidi* 641) who prize whatever lurks beneath the surface of *inuersis uerbis* (642) – contorted phraseology, enigmatic expressions, or both – that possess a pleasing sound. *Stolidi* is commonly read as a calque for *Stoici*, and this interpretation makes sense. It was certainly characteristic of the Stoa to search for meaning within language, lurking beneath the surface of words, as Lucretius says, even if addiction to mellifluous sonorities for their own sake seems out of sorts with Stoic ascesis. It is

----

[19] Snyder (1980), 117.

worth noting, however, that if Lucretius does mean to bash the Stoics in particular here, then he does so by means of the very method he ridicules. Rendering *Stoici* as *Stolidi* parodies the Stoic method of finding the "true names" of things, the ἔτυμοι λόγοι, that lurk beneath the surface of language. As in the case of Heraclitus' name, moreover, this ironic etymologizing involves translation from Greek into Latin. This idea is in fact hinted at in the phrase *inuersis uerbis* (642), which I have rendered variously above as "jumble of words," "contorted phraseology," and "enigmatic expressions." It might also be rendered as "in translation": the *stolidi* admire all the more things that they find expressed in the decent obscurity of a learned language – which means, for Lucretius, in Greek. It is as if the true meaning of things could be only dimly adumbrated in Greek – as if any word or idea, in order to disclose its real meaning and be completely understood, demystified, and perhaps even exposed as fraudulent or mistaken, had to be translated into Latin.

If this is correct, then it makes sense to return to Heraclitus' name and consider its first element. Among the Stoics the name of the goddess Ἥρα was thought to be connected etymologically with ἀήρ: "air," but also a substance that conceals or obscures things from view, such as the mist in which Homer's Athena wraps Odysseus. In a passage that mocks Stoic etymologizing, this interpretation would make sense. Line 638 begins with Heraclitus' name; the line that follows begins with a mocking etymology, *clarus ob obscuram linguam*, "famous for his foggy manner of expression" – again, an "etymology" that entails translation from Greek into Latin. The very sound of Lucretius' rendering – the deliberately awkward repetition of *ob*, the heavy-handed rhyme of *-am* – depend on the sonic resources of Lucretius' Latin, which is revealed as a medium uniquely able to disclose the "etymological truth" lurking beneath the Greek names of Ἡράκλειτος and οἱ Στωϊκοί and thus to expose them to the ridicule that they deserve.

We see then that Lucretius' latinate punning asserts a contrast between his first two exempla: where Heraclitus is ironically *clarus*, Empedocles, like Lucretius, is *carus*. Heraclitus' fame is situated *inter Graios* (and among the *inanis* rather than the *grauis Graios* at that), while Empedocles' proximity to Lucretius is stressed in philosophical, geographical, ethnographic, and linguistic terms. Following Heraclitus

the near-barbarian and Empedocles the near-Latin we find Anaxagoras.
Here the contrast between the sheer linguistic materiality of Latin and
Greek reaches an extreme:

> Nunc et Anaxagorae scrutemur homoeomerian
> quam Grai memorant nec nostra dicere lingua
> concedit nobis patrii sermonis egestas,
> sed tamen ipsam rem facile est exponere uerbis.

> And now let us scrutinize what the Greeks call Anaxagoras' ὁμοιο-
> μέρεια, which the poverty of our ancestral speech does not permit us
> to say in our own language, though the thing itself is easy to explain
> in words.   1.830–33

The first line of this passage plays on the contrasting sonic textures of
the two languages: the closed vowels and the monosyllables of *nunc* and
et together with the sharp consonantal clusters of *scrutemur* set off the
smooth, polysyllabic orotundity of *Anaxagorae* and *homoeomerian*.[20]
The beauty of these Greek words lies beyond the frontier of poor latinity; but the idea (*ipsam rem*) is perfectly easy to express in words
(*uerbis*). This quite interesting expression seems to suggest that *homoeomeria* actually is not a word, or that Greek words are not really words,
or that *uerba* – i.e. Latin words – are the only ones that count. At any
rate, Lucretius continues to contrast the mellifluous sound of Anaxagoras' technical terminology with very informal and none-too-elegant
Latin diction:

> Principio, rerum quam dicit homoeomerian,
> ossa uidelicet e pauxillis atque minutis
> ossibus hic et de pauxillis atque minutis
> uisceribus uiscus gigni sanguenque creari
> sanguinis inter se multis coeuntibu' guttis
> ex aurique putat micis consistere posse
> aurum et de terris terram consistere paruis,
> ignibus ex ignis, umorem umoribus esse,
> cetera consimili fingit ratione putatque.

---

[20] Denis Feeney remarks that "*homoeomeria* [in this passage] and *harmonia* [at
3.100–31; cf. 4.1248] are the only technical philosophical terms of Greek that
[Lucretius] transliterates." On the argument at this point see Wardy (1988), 126.

First, as for what he calls ὁμοιομέρεια in things, well, he thinks that bones come from little tiny bones, and flesh from little tiny fleshes, and that blood is made when many drops of blood gather together, and that gold can come out of little flecks of gold, and earth congeal from little earths, fire from fires, water from waters, and he imagines and thinks all other things by the same reasoning.   1.834–42

Here Lucretius returns to the same kind of sonic contrast that we found in the preceding lines: against the Greek abstraction *homoeomerian*, "the principle of like-partedness," we now have the unpretentious Latin *ossa*, "bones," followed by the prosaic words *uidelicet*, *pauxillis*, and *minutis*. To increase the impression of meager resources, Lucretius actually repeats these words in consecutive lines that sound nearly identical:

ossa uidel*ic*et **e pauxillis atque minutis**

ossibus h*ic* **et** de **pauxillis atque minutis**

This pattern continues throughout the passage in the pairing of *uisceribus uiscus*, *terris terram*, *ignibus ex ignis*, *umorem umoribus* and in the repetition of *putat* (839, 842). Two things are accomplished. First, Lucretius' down-to-earth Latin exposes Anaxagoras' polysyllabic Greek technical term as pretentious. Second, Lucretius has been illustrating "how much elements can do by just changing their order" (*tantum elementa queunt permutato ordine solo*, 827), where *elementa* is the *mot juste* for both atoms and letters of the alphabet. The same Lucretian *elementa*, we will shortly learn (1.907–10), can produce wood (*lignum*) and fire (*ignis*) and can explain how it is that there are elements of fire lurking within wood.[21] Between lines 839 and 842 the elements change hardly at all, reflecting the fact that Anaxagoras does not believe in atoms, but holds that everything, no matter how small you cut it, will always look the same. Lucretius' language here thus accurately reflects Anaxagoras' theory and reveals its lack of explanatory power: all it can tell us is that bones are made of bones. Here let us remember that this very passage invokes the motif of *patrii sermonis egestas*, and note that the deployment of this phrase in effect predicts the rhetorical stratagem that the poet will use to debunk the specious reasoning concealed

----

[21] Snyder (1980), especially 31–51.

behind Anaxagoras' hifalutin philosophical terminology. Is Lucretius, then, as a philosopher or as a poet, limited by the poverty of his ancestral speech?

To answer this question we should consider the meaning of "poverty" both in Epicurus' philosophy and in Latin culture. In the first place, it seems clear that if Lucretius depends at all on an equation between the ideas of poverty and inadequacy, he does so with great irony, alluding to this attitude in order to drive home his own assertion that he, writing in Latin, has bettered his Greek models in specifically linguistic terms. Lucretius' apparently apologetic tone when he speaks of the "poverty" of his native tongue is belied by the linguistic resources that Latin affords him to improve on the efforts of previous, Greek philosophers. The unique suitability of Latin to express both the grandeur of Lucretius' theme and the technical realities of his exposition is an idea that recurs over and over again, even if the poet handles it with extreme tact. The famous illustration of the parallel between atoms and letters of the alphabet is an important instance. We know, of course, that Epicurus himself spoke of the elements or *stoicheia* both of the physical universe and of the philosophical system that he developed to describe it. The remains of his work are so fragmentary that we cannot say with certainty that he did not use an alphabetic illustration of the type we have just seen in Lucretius. But we can observe how successful Lucretius' illustration is, and conclude that it is either an impressively apt piece of original argumentation or else a brilliant translation into Latin of a similar illustration, now lost, but previously made by Epicurus in Greek. Either way it is clear that the "poverty" of Lucretius' Latin does not prevent him from matching and perhaps even surpassing the master's exploitation of perceived parallelisms between philosophical truth and linguistic forms. In fact, the supposed restriction of linguistic resources available to the Latin poet actually suggests the exiguous range of material resources out of which the Epicurean universe is composed, much better, in fact, than does the embarrassment of riches that the Greek language lavishes upon those who speak and write it. In his doxography Lucretius systematically debunks the idea that Greek is superior to Latin as a medium for poetry and philosophy on every score: its supposedly greater beauty and mellifluous qualities, its larger vocabulary, the ease with which it forms compounds, its capacity for subtle philosophical expression, all are revealed as traps that lead to obscurity, muddled thinking, silliness. Even the geographical extension of the language is turned to its disadvantage, except as westward colonization has brought about proximity to Lucretius' own linguistic domain. The "poverty" of Latin is thus revealed as a positive advantage.

We tend to take Lucretius' disclaimer about "poverty" too literally, to interpret it simplistically, and to believe in it implicitly; but we should not. For that matter, we should be careful of assuming too easily that poverty does in fact connote inadequacy. In Epicurus' and therefore Lucretius' ethical system it is strongly asserted that human wants are few, that luxury corrupts and debilitates. In Latin culture too the praise of an unassuming, even a hardscrabble way of life is a constant theme, representing almost an article of faith. When Lucretius refers to the poverty of the Latin language that forces him to work hard at finding the right words to convey Epicurus' message, there is no reason to assume that he sees the poem he has labored to write as second best. In producing a Latin *De rerum natura*, Lucretius was not attempting to supply a surrogate *Peri phuseos* but rather to improve on the original as only the specific resources of the Latin language would allow him to do. Even Epicurus, forced to contend with the luxuriance of the Greek tongue, could not find a form adequate to his message; this task was left to his greatest disciple, who was also one of the greatest masters of Latin speech.

The gender of Latin

No Latin Sappho

To translate Lucretius' duplicitous phrase as "the poverty of our ancestral speech" is to introduce a second duplicity: the Latin refers not to "ancestral" but to "paternal" speech (***patrii*** *sermonis egestas*). This specificity might mean less if it were not common to speak of English as one's "mother tongue." In fact, we are dealing with a phenomenon that goes well beyond these two phrases in these two languages, one that involves an extremely widespread problematic whereby classical speech is gendered masculine and vernacular speech is gendered feminine.

The phenomenon is not confined to latinity or even to language as such. In traditional European culture, the life of the mind and of *belles-lettres* in general was considered until fairly recently the almost exclusive domain of men, regardless of what language they used. Isidore of Seville writes that "there is no feminine form of the word 'author'."[1] Isidore's point is purely grammatical but, as often, grammatical considerations are emblematic of larger concerns. Mary Ann Evans' decision to publish under the name George Eliot indicates clearly that many centuries later the author function was still gendered masculine. Similarly, within Eliot's own work and that of her contemporaries we find evidence that the cultural space defined by facility with Latin remained a largely male preserve and one from which they implicitly exclude themselves.[2]

The point here is that the feminine gender of vernacular speech is

---

[1] *"auctorem" autem femineo genere dici non posse* (*Orig.* 10.1.2).

[2] I will discuss this point in ch. 4.

constructed as the defining opposite of masculine, classical speech. This attitude appears in many cultures. In the Jewish tradition, for example, it was not uncommon to regard Hebrew as a "masculine language," that is the exclusive province of scholarly men, and Yiddish as a "feminine" language of untutored women. This gendering of language corresponded to a gendering of space: witness the frequent designation (and denigration) of Yiddish as the "mother tongue" (*mama loshn*), a language spoken in the kitchen, in contrast with Hebrew, the "holy tongue" (*leshnon hagodesh*) that was read in the study or chanted in *shul*.[3] At the same time, the prerogative by which any linguistic culture may claim for itself association with the "preferred gender" disappears whenever that same language is viewed from a different linguistic and cultural perspective. The vernacular culture of the Middle Ages and Renaissance viewed Latin, Greek, and Hebrew as fundamentally different from the vernacular, finding in the existence of these *tres linguae sacrae* an image of perfection and proof of divine providence. From a Latin perspective, however, the distinctive properties of each language provided an opportunity to parse their relationship in terms of gender. An anonymous commentator from St. Gall observes that "a neuter in Greek, a feminine in Hebrew, and a masculine in Latin, [the spirit] remains steadfast in the same meaning; it remains steadfast in all genders, whether pronounced as *pneuma, ruha*, or *flatus*."[4] Within this satisfying arrangement lies the potential for further comfort in the fact that only the Latin word for "spirit" is of the masculine gender.

In the modern period both Latin and Greek are masculine with respect to English; but in Roman antiquity, Latin claims the masculine and regularly attempts to feminize the Greek. Horace famously figures the relationship in explicitly gendered terms:

> Graecia capta ferum uictorem cepit et artes
> intulit agresti Latio....   *Epistles* 2.1.156–57

Greece here is a captive woman who has fallen into the possession of a victorious, Latin-speaking, male conqueror. A captive herself, she has

---

[3] Hellerstein (1990); for a more general view Seidman (1997).

[4] *grece neutrum, ebraice femineum, latine masculinum | in uirtute pari uiget | "pneuma," "ruha," "flatus" uiget omnigenis uocitatus.* Text and discussion in Berschin (1988), 150.

turned the tables on her master and "taken" him as well (*cepit* 156), much as Propertius says Cynthia was the first to "take" him (*cepit* 1.1.1). The image of the captive woman who captures her captor is cognate with that of the elegiac mistress – the *domina*, a woman of Greek name and servile or libertine status who nevertheless "enslaves" and "rules" her Latin, freeborn, citizen lover.

The connection within the Latin cultural imaginary between women's voices and the Greek language is strengthened by an important fact of literary history. We know of many more women writing in Greek than in Latin. This bald statement may be misleading: we can also name many more men writing in Greek than in Latin. But the Greeks could point to Sappho, who was revered as one of their greatest cultural heroes, a figure fully comparable to Pindar, Anacreon, and her country-man Alcaeus – even, according to a common conceit, a tenth muse.[5] The existence of a woman poet who wrote during one of the earliest periods of Greek literary history and left a large body of work that was universally recognized as canonical, is a matter of colossal significance. It does not mean that the study of ancient Greek would not for much of the modern period be a predominantly masculine pursuit. It does not mean that the question of Sappho's own sexuality would not be an issue of persistent, absorbing interest to later generations. Sappho's poetry has always been a locus of contestation between the individual feminine voice and the collective masculinist discourse that limits and threatens to occlude it. Nor does the existence and position of Sappho and other women writers mean that ancient Greek culture was anything other than overwhelmingly misogynist in its dominant ideological structures. The gender of Greek is a problem unto itself. But Sappho's voice has never fallen silent: it has always been there in its irreducible quiddity, singing in distinctive counterpoint to the masculine voice, now harmonious, now dissonant. It has given rise to imitators both direct and indirect: Cleobulina, Corinna, Telesilla, Praxilla, Erinna, Moero, Anyte, Hedyle, Nossis, Melinno. At least some work by all these poets survives; but we have hardly any writing by Roman women – one of the few whose work we have, Julia Balbilla, actually composed in Sappho's Aeolic Greek dialect instead of Latin – and in Rome as well as in Greece literary women are compared not to some founding heroine of

[5] See, e.g., *Anth. Pal.* 9.506.

feminine latinity, but to Sappho herself. There is no Latin Sappho. If any further proof of this statement were required, we would find it in the simple fact that the most convincing candidates for the title *Sappho Latina* are both men. First Catullus, then Ovid staked his claim to the title, each in his own way ventriloquizing Sappho.[6] For Horace to acknowledge her as a model for his own poetry, he must comment on her transgressive behavior by calling her *mascula Sappho* (*Epist.* 1.19.28). Commentators are divided over whether her sexuality or her chosen career is at issue here; we can hardly do other than keep both points in mind. As the archetypal woman writer, Sappho was regarded as both sexually and socially transgressive, especially at Rome. The simple but important fact is that no woman writing in prose or in poetry ever achieved a stature among the Latins remotely comparable to Sappho's among the Greeks. Her lack of a true Latin counterpart attests the degree to which Latin language and Latin culture cleave to the masculine gender.

Alongside the discursive construct by which an entire language may be gendered as "masculine" or "feminine," as in the phrases *patrius sermo* and "mother tongue," there is the more tangible issue of whether masculine and feminine speech actually differ from one another within a given language. Let us assume that male is to female as Latin is to English; is it also the case that women's speech differs from that of men in both Latin and English? And does the speech of women differ from that of men in both languages in the same way?

If we begin to address the question from the perspective of the vernacular, about which we have more abundant and varied information, the answer seems clear. Empirically, linguists have indeed found and documented quite definite differences between men's and women's speech with respect to vocabulary, syntax, intonation, and other factors.[7] Theoretically, several influential scholars have carefully articulated the notion of women's writing (Cixous' *écriture feminine*, Irigaray's *parler femme*) to explain these differences as they pertain to literature.[8] If we can assume that Latin speakers behave more or less like speakers of

---

[6] Harvey (1989); DeJean (1989), 43–115, esp. 60–78.

[7] Lakoff (1975); Bodine (1975).

[8] Richlin (1993) and Gold (1993) are useful entrees into the considerable literature on this topic, clarifying the relationship between feminist theory and practical criticism of ancient texts with respect to the female voice.

English, we should therefore expect to find real differences between masculine and feminine latinity.

Our ancient sources generally regard women as poor speakers, whether judging them by their rhetorical style or by their sheer latinity. Women talk too fast; they do not take the trouble to distinguish their syllables clearly; they leave things out. What they manage to stammer out is badly phrased. It is all emotion, no reason. In rhetorical theory, these perceived deficiencies became prescriptive under some circumstances. Marcus Cornelius Fronto recommends to his pupil the emperor Marcus Aurelius particular models in different stylistic categories. Novius and Pomponius, writers of Atellan farce, are good at imitating rustic speech; Lucilius the satirist handles well the technical argot of various trades; and Titus Quinctius Atta, the author of *fabulae togatae*, "excelled in women's language."[9] Though the surviving fragments of Atta's oeuvre contain no indication of what Fronto meant, it seems clear that some readers, at any rate, recognized distinctions of gender in the Latin poetic voice. Modern research as well has found that the women of Latin comedy speak differently from the men, and the distinctions that have been found involve, precisely, various tokens of emotionalism, inarticulate exclamations, and the like.[10] What this means, however, is not that we can extract from such data firm conclusions about the character of feminine latinity, but merely that we have some evidence about the ways in which male authors represented female speech.

The actual corpus of women's writing from Roman times is heartbreakingly small. The few scraps of Latin we have that were certainly written by a woman's own hand are found in the correspondence of Sulpicia Lepidina, which contains at least two letters from her friend Claudia Severa. Both women had accompanied their husbands to military outposts in northern Britain at about AD 100.[11] The letters are effusive and affectionate, different in style if not language from the businesslike military letters with which they were found, but not so different

---

[9] *Nam praeter hos partim scriptorum animaduertas particulatim elegantes, Nouium et Pomponium et id genus in uerbis rusticanis et iocularibus ac ridiculariis, Attam in muliebribus, Sisennam in lasciuis, Lucilium in cuiusque artis ac negotii propriis (ad M. Caesarem 4.3.2).*

[10] Adams (1984), with further references.

[11] Text and commentary in Bowman and Thomas (1994), 256–65 (#291–94).

from the more personal letters of Cicero and Pliny. Another Sulpicia left a body of poetry that has been transmitted to us under the name of Tibullus. Not until 1838 did scholars generally recognize five or six poems (3.13–18) as the work of neither Tibullus nor of yet a third Sulpicia, the poet Sulpicia Caleni (whom we shall discuss shortly), but of a young woman generally identified as the niece of M. Valerius Messalla, patron of Tibullus and several other poets of the Augustan period.[12] At first no one thought Sulpicia worth reading except as a curiosity, the only surviving female poet of Latin antiquity. Indeed, it was in connection with the discovery of her work that the very concept of feminine latinity gained some modern currency. Even scholars who disparaged the idea of a distinctively feminine latinity *per se* described Sulpicia's style in condescendingly gendered terms.[13] But Sulpicia is now taken more seriously. Indeed, as the critical condescension that her sex attracted gave way to more even-handed appreciative efforts, Sulpicia came to be seen not only as a serious and original poet, but an uncommonly tough-minded one given to measured, highly-involved, and rather complex modes of expression. As she was taken more seriously, scholars began to find in her just the opposite qualities to those that their predecessors had put down to "feminine latinity."[14] And, necessarily, this line of inquiry has brought us to a point where it is worth asking again whether we can believe implicitly that Sulpicia's poetry is in fact the work of a Roman woman.[15] By the same token, when Ovid (*Tr.* 3.7) addresses a young protégée whom he calls Perilla, and whom he elsewhere seems to identify with a Metella (*Tr.* 2.437–38), is he disclosing a valuable testimonium about an otherwise unknown woman poet? Or is this open letter from exile about the dangers of a literary career more an imaginative exercise in poetic self-fashioning than a piece of historical evidence? The alternatives may not be mutually exclusive; a large part of Ovid's genius consists in managing to have it both ways. But it is certainly possible that Perilla is no more than the projection of a male writer inclined to see in their relative powerlessness an affinity between the poet's lot and that of the female sex.

[12] On this point and on the question of attribution in general see Parker (1994).

[13] Smith (1913), 77–87, especially 80–85.

[14] Hinds (1987); Lowe (1988); Parker (1994).

[15] Holzberg (1999).

At this point our two lines of inquiry converge. The historical project of recovering the language of Roman women is greatly complicated by the theoretical project of coming to terms with the cultural significance of gender in Latin literature. The feminine voice embodied in the words of actual women speaking and writing in Latin has been all but silenced by the discursive construction that regards Latin as the language of men. It is as if the *patrius sermo* could not allow for those internal distinctions with respect to gender that we can observe within the "mother tongue" – as if it were a property of the masculine language to occlude feminine speech altogether, in contrast to feminine languages, within which distinct patterns of male and female speech can coexist. But the possibility of recovering at least some sense of women's Latin should not be dismissed, if only because to do so is to surrender to the circular logic whereby classical Latin constructs itself as masculine speech by simply denying and silencing the feminine voice. A part of our effort to recover this voice will involve testing the definition of "the classical." At the same time, it will be necessary to explore as fully as possible the gendering of Latin as a discursive construct.

Mothers and sons

Against pressing too closely the distinction between *patrius sermo* and "mother tongue" one might adduce Quintilian's advice in the opening chapters of his magnum opus:

> I should prefer [the rising orator's] parents to have as much eloquence as possible, and I am not speaking only of fathers: we are informed that the Gracchi were indebted for their eloquence in large measure to their mother, Cornelia, whose extremely cultivated speech has been bequeathed to posterity as well in the form of letters. Gaius Laelius' daughter is said to have recalled in conversation her father's elegant style, and the oration of Quintus Hortensius' daughter that was delivered before the triumvirs continues to be read not merely in consideration of her sex.[16]

---

[16] *In parentibus uero quam plurimum esse eruditionis optauerim. Nec de patribus tantum loquor: nam Gracchorum eloquentiae multum contulisse accepimus Corneliam matrem, cuius doctissimus sermo in posteros quoque est epistulis traditus, et Laelia C. filia reddidisse in loquendo paternam elegantiam dicitur, et Hortensiae Q. filiae oratio apud triumuiros habita legitur non tantum in sexus honorem (IO 1.1.6).*

The prominence of mothers here might raise expectations that will not be met. After stressing their importance, Quintilian has little to say about mothers or any other women in the rest of his work. Indeed, actual Roman women appear with less frequency than do mythological heroines. Most frequently women are named in connection with a speech that some male orator delivered for or against them in a legal proceeding. Often enough they serve merely to illustrate a degrading stereotype: Clodia sleeps around (9.2.99), Domitia spends too much (6.3.74), Fabia lies about her age (6.3.73), Sasia seduces her son-in-law (4.2.105). Celsina is a *potens femina*; in one case she was named as a supporter by the opponents of Domitius Afer, one of Quintilian's oratorical mentors. His strategy? Ridicule her retainers by pretending to think she must be a man (6.3.85). Better to be like Cloatilla, a Roman Antigone whom the same Afer defended against a charge of burying her dead husband after he had taken part in a rebellion. His argument? She was acting not out of principle, but as a confused and helpless woman: "In her fear, the lady did not know what she could legally do, what honor her husband deserved" (9.2.20). The position of the Roman woman in Quintilian's universe is actually far from what he implies by stressing the importance of the mother in the orator's early training. That position is summed up by the predicament of Marcia, the woman whom Cato the younger divorced so that he might lend her out in a dynastic marriage to Quintus Hortensius, father of the aforementioned lady pleader. Twice Quintilian mentions Marcia, both times with reference to the *controversia* topic of whether Cato ought to have taken this action (3.5.11–13, 10.5.13); nowhere does he or any other writer consider whether Marcia herself ought to have spoken against the plan.

Women, then, are almost entirely written out of Quintilian's book: we must take literally his ideal, for which he claims the elder Cato as source, of the orator as a *uir bonus dicendi peritus*, "a good *man* skilled at speaking" (*IO* 12.1.1; cf. 1 *pr.* 9 *et passim*). But at least the first woman he mentions is one universally admired for her character and her culture: Cornelia Gracchi, daughter of Scipio Africanus and mother of the revolutionary tribunes Tiberius and Gaius Gracchus. Cornelia is the first Roman woman whom we know to have been educated in *belles-lettres*. She is in fact one of the first to emerge from our sources with something like a personality, narrowly escaping the usual fate of her predecessors and many of her successors – to serve as a mere emblem of virtue or of vice. In many ways she remains altogether exceptional; but it is she, if anyone, who occupies the foundational and, in some respects, the normative position of the Latin literary woman.

Quintilian cites Cornelia's letters in particular as documents attesting her eloquence, the eloquence that was her particular contribution to the education of her sons; and if anyone were capable of representing Latin as the "mother tongue" it would be she. Cicero makes this image almost explicit when he says, "I have read the letters of Cornelia, mother of the Gracchi, and her sons appear to have been raised not at their mother's breast, but in her conversation."[17] I would give a lot to know just what Cicero found in the style of the speeches of Tiberius and Gaius Gracchus to remind him of their mother's style. Part of the story is not only that Cornelia was a cultivated stylist herself, but that her husband was "a thoughtful, serious fellow, but hardly eloquent."[18] Both sons were gifted speakers and in this respect, at least, took after their mother. Would Cornelia's legacy to her sons have been remembered if their father had been even a tolerably good speaker? Or is the strength of a mother's contribution in these matters proportional to the father's weakness? Elsewhere Cicero stresses the fact that Cornelia was careful to have her son Gaius educated in Greek by the best available teachers.[19] The "mother tongue" of native Latin eloquence thus reveals itself, by a familiar pattern, as something derived from imported models.

In view of how little remains from the speeches of the two brothers, it is hard to form any specific opinion about what their eloquence may have owed to their mother. Is there in fact anything to suggest that the Roman woman most famous for her literary culture contributed to the language anything of herself or of her sex? Does Cornelia represent a feminine voice in Latin culture, and did she pass some part of that voice on to her sons?

It happens that we possess two fragments that are supposed to be from letters written by Cornelia to her younger son Gaius – examples,

---

[17] *legimus epistulas Corneliae matris Gracchorum: apparet filios non tam in gremio educatos quam in sermone matris* (*Brutus* 211).

[18] *homo prudens et grauis, haudquaquam eloquens* (*De orat.* 1.38).

[19] *Fuit [C.] Gracchus diligentia Corneliae matris a puero doctus et Graecis litteris eruditus. Nam semper habuit exquisitos e Graecia magistros, in eis iam adulescens Diophanem Mytilenaeum Graeciae temporibus illis disertissimum* (*Brutus* 104).

therefore, of the very letters that Quintilian and Cicero praise. The fragments are preserved in a manuscript containing the works of Cornelia's distant kinsman, Cornelius Nepos, and are short enough to be quoted in full:

> Words from a letter of Cornelia, mother of the Gracchi, excerpted from Cornelius Nepos' book on Latin historians: "You will say that it is a fine thing to take revenge upon one's enemies. It seems no greater and finer a thing to anyone than to me, but only if it can be pursued without danger to the republic. But in as much as that cannot be, for a long time and in many areas our enemies will not perish and will be just as they now are, rather than that the republic should be afflicted and perish." The same letter in another passage: "I would not be afraid to swear a formal oath that, apart from those who murdered Tiberius Gracchus, no one has given me as much pain and trouble as you have about this – you ought to have taken the part of all the children I have ever had and taken care that I should have the least possible trouble in my old age, and that whatever you do be intended to please me, and that you consider it wicked to undertake any significant action against my advice – especially now, when so little time is left me. Can you not indulge even that brief moment without opposing me and harassing the republic? How will it all end? Will our family ever stop raving? Can there ever be a limit to this affair? Will we ever stop having and causing trouble? Will you ever grow ashamed of disrupting and disturbing the republic? But if this simply cannot be, wait until I am dead, *then* run for tribune. You may do as you like, for all I care, when I will not know about it. When I am dead, you will worship me and invoke me, your parent, as a god: at that time will you not be embarrassed to petition those gods whom you betrayed and abandoned in life and in the flesh? May Jupiter not permit you to persist in this nor allow such madness to enter your heart; and if you do persist, I fear that for the rest of your life you will feel such pain for what you have done that you will never, ever be able to find happiness."[20]

One of the most common observations about these letters concerns Cornelia's status as parent and involves gender in a very explicit sense.

[20] The Latin text (Nepos fr. 59 Marshall) is printed in the appendix to this volume.

In the longer passage, the writer refers to herself as the "parent" or *parens* of her addressee. The word attracts notice for two reasons. First, *parens* is not quite synonymous with *mater*; and second, by assuming the title of *parens*, the writer suddenly, if briefly, refers to herself in the masculine gender. Why does Cornelia style herself in this peculiar way?

It is true that *parentes* corresponds generally to "parents" in English (and contains something of the French *parents* as well). In the singular, however, *parens* is a common synonym for "father."[21] It is found in poetry as a grandiloquent substitute for *mater*, but normally in a metaphorical sense and when there is no particular father in view.[22] A woman is seldom called *parens*, which might even be paired with and contrasted to "mother," as in Propertius' *ossa tibi iuro per **matris** et ossa **parentis*** (2.20.15). This situation is of course rather odd. Most scholars agree with Isidore (*Orig.* 9.4.5) in connecting *parens* with *pario*, which normally means "to bear (offspring)" and only exceptionally appears in the sense of "beget." It can be used in a metaphorical sense: Augustus provides an apt illustration in his slogan *pax **parta** terra marique* (*Res gestae* 13), where the passive voice preserves the image of childbirth without actually assigning the roles of mother and father. In this usage, masculine achievements in the social sphere are implicitly equated with women's ability to give birth. Nowhere is the male's awe and envy of the female's biological role more evident than here. It is related to this awe and envy, I suggest, and remarkable in any case that *parens* normally means "father" rather than "mother."[23]

By styling herself as *parens* Cornelia makes a different point than if she had written *mater*. Observe the sentence in which the word appears: ***parentabis** mihi et inuocabis deum **parentem***. Here is a piece of rhetorical display, the *figura etymologica*. We expect such colors from a lady famed for her literary culture. But this display performs the additional work of activating the religious sphere: Cornelia as *parens* will, after her death, be eligible to receive cult from her wayward son. She thus represents herself as something more than Gaius' biological mother and lays

---

[21] E.g. Cicero *Diu. Caec.* 61, *Balb.* 11, *Red. Sen.* 37; Lucretius *DRN* 2.1167; Caesar *BC* 1.74.6; Virgil *Aen.* 1.75; Livy 4.17.9; Augustus *RG* 2; etc.

[22] E.g. Virgil *Geo.* 2.173; Ovid *Ib.* 455; Statius *Theb.* 3.134; cf. Pliny *NH* 7.1 (of *natura*).

[23] This point has been thoroughly investigated by Odgers (1928).

claim to the full institutional authority of parenthood, an authority invested principally in the *paterfamilias*. Here however we can glimpse the limits of Cornelia's claim. Gaius' father is dead. Were he alive, he could at least in principle have exercised a father's right and ordered his son to desist from any course of action that displeased him. The elder Tiberius Gracchus was no man of words, but that did not matter: it needed no eloquence to impose the *patria potestas*. But with his father's death, Gaius became his own man. Cornelia marshaled all the forces of her eloquence to claim what she could of her deceased husband's authority; yet the very effort and the means she used themselves betray the fact that this authority was not hers, that she was not a *paterfamilias* at all.

There is still a further point. The reading *deum* (and not *deam*) is secure. Cornelia thus treats *parens* as a word of masculine gender. This usage agrees with her attempt to play a socially masculine role. But the grammatical tradition has something to say about this word as well and, interestingly, provides the one tangible example we have of an affinity between Cornelia's latinity and that of her son. Charisius informs us that "Heir', 'parent', and 'person', though understood with respect to either sex, are nevertheless always of masculine gender. No one ever says 'the second heiress' or 'a good parentess' or 'a bad personess', but uses only the masculine even though a woman may be in question." Notice how Charisius recalls the aforementioned notice of Isidore on the masculine gender of the word *auctor*. This is an intriguing list of words – "author," "heir," "parent," "person" – for which Latin has no feminine form. Again there is a congruency between the rules of grammar and the social constructs to which these grammatical concepts refer.

At this point the text is disturbed, but the crucial points are quite clear. First we find a citation from Pacuvius' tragedy *Medus*, in which the hero invokes the sun's aid as he searches for Medea, "my parent" (the Latin is *mei parentis*). Charisius then cites one of the Gracchi – probably Gaius, who appears much more frequently than his brother in the grammatical tradition – as another authority for this usage. "But Gracchus says 'he loves his parents' (*suos parentes*) when he means 'mother'." This information is followed by an extremely tantalizing lacuna of unknown extent, and then by a citation of "another letter" in which someone, evidently a woman, announces "I am your parent" in

63

the form *tuus parens sum.* There is no telling precisely what information was lost in that lacuna, but it is difficult not to believe that the woman in question – for the writer now must be a woman or the citation has no point – is Cornelia, mother of the Gracchi, and that the letter was very similar to the one cited above.[24]

If these inferences are right, here is at least one very definite point of resemblance between Cornelia's latinity and that of her sons. The orators shared with their mother a respect for the linguistic rules governing such things as grammatical gender even where these conflicted with the logical and mimetic properties of language. It only makes sense that *parens*, like *coniunx* ("spouse"), should be treated as a noun of common gender. Eventually this was to be the case in general usage; but an element of conservatism resisted this development and continued to note in technical treatises the way things had been before.

Cornelia's influence on her sons' latinity is resonant with cultural significance. Her grammatically constructed language resists the sense construction that eventually made *parens* a word of common gender. Not to treat the word as feminine when it refers to a woman was, perhaps, old-fashioned even in Cornelia's day. For a woman to do so when speaking of herself is doubly surprising. In aftertimes this usage was considered archaic and was connected specifically with the language of Cornelia and her son.[25] Reading the fragments of her letters or of her sons' speeches we can understand this tradition: their language is rather archaic, a point that comes out also in orthography (*lubet* for *libet*), in usage (the future imperatives *petito* and *facito* instead of the present-tense equivalents *pete* and *fac*, in *deum* for *deorum*), and in certain ornamental effects (e.g. the alliterative cadence of *uti in nullo tempore tute tibi placere possis*). Archaism of course is not intrinsically related to considerations of gender. But there are indications that some ancient

---

[24] Charisius *Ars* I : 130–31 Barwick = 102–03 Keil; Pacuvius fr. trag. 219 Ribbeck[3]; C. Gracchus fr. 67 Malcovati.

[25] Paul the Deacon's epitome of Festus, *De uerborum significatu,* observes that "when the ancients called even a mother a 'parent', they used the masculine gender," and he continues with another citation of Gracchus: "they said 'cross' in the masculine gender, as in Gracchus' 'he deserved to die a painful death'" (*masculino genere parentem appellabant antiqui etiam matrem; masculino genere dicebant crucem, ut est illud Gracchi: "dignus fuit qui malo cruce periret,"* Pauli exc. Festi p. 137.16 Lindsay).

authorities in fact did conceive of an ideal association between archaism and a specific type of feminine latinity, a type that respected and embodied the linguistic *mos maiorum* by faithfully preserving the traditions and character of the *patrius sermo.*

Fathers and daughters

Cornelia's followers – those whose names we know – are few, and in general present us with much the same image of feminine latinity. These are women who are noble, austere, dignified, and almost masculine in their linguistic culture. One of these is Laelia, daughter of Gaius Laelius Sapiens, a woman whose conversation, Quintilian tells us, recalled her father's eloquence. Laelia's role is thus the converse of Cornelia's: where Cornelia passes her eloquence down to her sons, Laelia receives hers from her father. Cicero in his dialogue *De oratore* recounts an anecdote concerning Laelia, and it is no doubt this passage that Quintilian has in mind.

The narrator of Cicero's anecdote about Laelia is the orator Lucius Licinius Crassus, whose general subject is pure latinity. If one is to speak Latin, Crassus declares, one must take care to use impeccable diction, observe proper distinctions of case, tense, gender, and number, and also control carefully the timbre of one's voice. "For there are certain faults that everybody wants to avoid: a voice that is soft or womanly or rather excessively odd-sounding or ridiculous. And there is also that fault which some people purposely cultivate: those rustics who affect a country accent, thinking that by this sound their speech better preserves the accent of the past."[26] I note in passing that these faults conform precisely to the collocation of special categories that Fronto invokes when advising Marcus Aurelius about sources of unusual diction. But a defender of Crassus (which is to say, of Cicero) might object that a feminine voice would sound odd or ridiculous only when coming from a man's mouth. This is indeed Crassus' main point. But by the usual logic, or rather, illogic, that obtains in gender construction, the

---

[26] *Sunt enim certa uitia, quae nemo est quin effugere cupiat: mollis uox aut muliebris aut quasi extra modum absona atque absurda. Est autem uitium, quod non nulli de industria consectantur: rustica uox et agrestis quosdam delectat, quom magis an- quitatem, si ita sonet, eorum sermo retinere uideatur (De orat. 3.41–42).*

reverse point is not true: we soon learn that a woman whose speech recalls that of men can be praised in no higher terms. Crassus continues, "Listening to Laelia, my mother-in-law – for women more easily keep old customs uncorrupted because, not being involved in conversations with many people, they more easily retain what they have first learned – listening to her, I say, I feel as though I were listening to Plautus or Naevius: the very sound of her voice is so straight and simple that it seems to involve no ostentation or imitation. And from this I infer that her father and ancestors spoke this way; not harshly, like the man I mentioned before, not sprawlingly, rudely, or gaspingly, but compactly and evenly and gently."[27] This wonderful passage limns an exceedingly circumscribed space within which feminine latinity can be said to – flourish? Hardly that. "Flourish" is much too forceful and prosperous a word for the retired and confined existence that Crassus allots to Laelia's voice. Even "exist" seems to allow Laelia more independence and autonomy than does her son-in-law. Feminine latinity in its preferred aspect is represented here as a mere echo of the masculine voice. Though Crassus says that there is nothing imitative in her speech, it is clear that what he values is no quality that Laelia possesses in her own right. Consider how the old woman is conceived: hearing her, Crassus declares, is like listening to a voice from the past. One occasionally does have this feeling when talking to certain old people, particularly those whose manners strike us as a bit old-fashioned and whose speech preserves a few turns of phrase that are in the process of being supplanted by a more up-to-date idiom without having yet become quaint. But Crassus describes the impression that Laelia makes in more extreme terms than these. His experience seems almost like what one feels in listening to an early phonograph recording – in fact, the span of time he mentions, between Plautus' day and his own, is about the same as the one that separates us from Edison. There is a sense in his account that Laelia is not fully envoiced; that she, like the phonograph, is not the

---

[27] *Equidem cum audio socrum meum Laeliam – facilius enim mulieres incorruptam antiquitatem conseruant, quod multorum sermonis expertes ea tenent semper, quae prima didicerunt – sed eam sic audio, ut Plautum mihi aut Naeuium uidear audire, sono ipso uocis ita recto et simplici est, ut nihil ostentationis aut imitationis adferre uideatur; ex quo sic locutum esse eius patrem iudico, sic maiores; non aspere ut ille, quem dixi, non uaste, non rustice, non hiulce, sed presse et aequabiliter et leniter (De or. 45).*

source of the utterance that Crassus hears, but rather a medium through which he gains access to the voice of Plautus, of Naevius, of Laelia's father, and of all her previous ancestors.

But again I must correct myself: not *all* her ancestors, but all her *male* ancestors are in question, and not *just* her ancestors, but the great writers of earlier generations as well. What is left in this of Laelia herself, of *her* voice? Nothing, in fact. It possesses no quality of its own. As a specimen of feminine latinity it is valued as much for its moral as for its linguistic qualities. The woman is an empty vessel, a receptacle for male seed or for male speech. If it is a sincere vessel, it will impart nothing of itself to its contents, but render up those contents unchanged, as pure and pristine as when they entered. Laelia's latinity is of this sort, a testament to her chastity and to her mother's. She inherits eloquence from her father and preserves it uncorrupted, serving as a repository or conduit of correct latinity handed down through her from grandfathers to grandsons. Her eloquence is a kind of dowry deriving from ancestral wealth that passes with her daughter's marriage into the possession of her son-in-law. And in Laelia's case, unlike Cornelia's, that treasure consists in nothing that could be adequately represented via the written word or indeed through another's voice: it is in the sound of her voice itself that the treasured idea of the *patrius sermo* consists, its timbre, its intensity, its precise intonation. These almost material aspects of Laelia's speech rather than anything she actually said, are all that mattered.

Not all daughters were as ideal examples of feminine latinity as Laelia. Quintilian's brief notice about Hortensia's eloquence is filled out by Valerius Maximus, who belongs to the same tradition. Hortensia is the daughter of Cicero's first great rival, the man whom he succeeded as the leading orator of his day. Unfortunately, neither of our sources says anything specific about Hortensia's latinity, and her speech does not survive.[28] But the moral of Hortensia's story in Valerius Maximus is much the same as that of Laelia's tale:

After the *matronae* had been burdened by the triumvirs with a heavy tax and none of their husbands dared to extend them his patronage, Hortensia, daughter of Quintus Hortensius, presented the ladies' case

---

[28] There is a Greek version in Appian *BC* 4.32–34.

before the triumvirs with constancy and favorable outcome. By re-producing her father's eloquence she succeeded in having the greater part of the assessment eliminated. Quintus Hortensius came back to life in the female line and breathed favor on his daughter's words; and if his male issue had been willing to follow her lead, the great legacy of Hortensian eloquence would not have come to an abrupt end in this lady's single court appearance.[29]

Cicero has nothing to say about this episode for the simple reason that he had died at the hands of the same triumvirs who passed this law. Hortensia's speech was obviously an act of courage as well as of elo-quence: when no man was willing to oppose the action of the triumvirs, she stood up to them and spoke against a kind of measure to which the male power structure had had frequent recourse throughout the Republic, a sumptuary tax levied specifically on women. She can hardly have had much, if any, experience speaking in public, particularly in a forensic setting. But speak she did, and with a success that not only met her immediate goal of reducing the tax, but, on Quintilian's testimony, actually assured her an approving readership in aftertimes. Valerius, like Quintilian, cites Hortensia's case with evident admiration. But his admiration for Hortensia herself is inscribed within a more general attitude of condescension towards, and even disapproval of, the female orator in general.

Valerius' condescension takes much the same form as we have seen in the case of Laelia. She was successful not because of her own merits, but because, like Laelia, she was the living repository of her father's talent. Again, as in the passage of *De oratore*, only more explicitly, latinity is represented as a paternal legacy that, when it passes into the female line, becomes an object of wonder to other men and a means of access to the exceptional and distinctive qualities of male ancestors, but ideally not a tool for which the woman herself finds practical application. In fact, Valerius cites Hortensia's coup almost as a reproach, not only to those

---

[29] *Hortensia uero Q. Hortensi filia, cum ordo matronarum graui tributo a triumuiris esset oneratus nec quicquam uirorum patrocinium eius accommodare auderet, cau-sam feminarum apud triumuiros et constanter et feliciter egit: repraesentata enim patris facundia impetrauit ut maior pars imperatae pecuniae his remitteretur. Reuixit tum muliebri stirpe Q. Hortensius uerbisque filiae aspirauit, cuius si uirilis sexus posteri uim sequi uoluissent, Hortensianae eloquentiae tanta hereditas una fe-minae actione abscissa non esset* (8.3.3).

men who failed to take up the cause of the *matronae*, but particularly to the great Hortensius' male descendants who allowed the tradition of *Hortensiana eloquentia* to meet an early and abrupt end (Valerius' word is *abscissa*, "cut short") in the exceptional and transgressive achievement of the orator's daughter.

Husbands and wives

Valerius Maximus' admiration for Hortensia is qualified somewhat by the company he makes her keep. Hers is the third and last *exemplum* in a brief chapter entitled "Women who have pled cases before magistrates on behalf of themselves or others," and his introduction to this topic resounds with disapproval: "I should certainly not remain silent about those ladies whose own silence in the forum and in the courts neither natural capacity nor the sense of restraint imposed by their station was sufficiently strong to maintain."[30] The story of Gaia Afrania, which immediately precedes that of Hortensia, is told in an unremittingly disapproving tone:

> Gaia Afrania, wife of the senator Licinius Bucco, was extremely litigious and often spoke before the praetor on her own behalf, not because she lacked advocates, but because she abounded in impudence. And so, by assiduously belaboring the court with a shrillness that was quite new to the forum she emerged as a most notorious emblem of womanish calumny, so much so that her name was hurled like an accusation against the vile character of women in general. She dragged out her existence until Gaius Caesar's second consulate, when his colleague was Publius Servilius. [I mention this because] it is the death of such a monster rather than its birth that should be remembered.[31]

---

[30] *Ne de his quidem feminis tacendum est, quas condicio naturae et uerecundia stolae ut in foro et iudiciis tacerent cohibere non ualuit* (8.3 praef.).

[31] *C. Afrania uero Licinii Bucconis senatoris uxor prompta ad lites contrahendas pro se semper apud praetores uerba fecit, non quod aduocatis deficiebatur, sed quod impudentia abundabat. Itaque inusitatis foro latratibus assidue tribunalia exercendo muliebris calumniae notissimum exemplum euasit, adeo ut pro crimine improbis feminarum moribus C. Afraniae nomen obiciatur. Prorogauit autem spiritum suum ad C. Caesarem iterum P. Seruilium consules: tale enim monstrum magis quo tempore extinctum quam quo sit ortum memoriae tradendum est* (8.3.2).

The example of Afrania does not obviate the respect that Valerius shows Hortensia, whom he styles by her full, aristocratic name, *Q. Hortensi filia*. Afrania's was a family of no great distinction, in oratory or otherwise; is this why she is named not as her father's daughter, but as her husband's wife, *uxor Licinii Bucconis senatoris*?[32] Hardly: Valerius is not concerned to enhance Afrania's prestige. Mentioning her husband is more likely a further piece of character assassination. Despite their senatorial rank, the Buccones, if we compare them to the Crassi, the Calvi, the Luculli, the Macri, or the Stolones, are hardly one of the more distinguished branches of the *gens Licinia*.[33] In fact, the word *bucco*, which is very rare, attracts particular attention: related to *bucca*, "cheek" or "mouth," it means "babbler," "drooler," or "dolt" and is found chiefly in comedy and related genres. Isidore of Seville glosses it as "garrulous, surpassing others in loquaciousness, but not in sense."[34] Latin of course is full of unflattering *cognomina*; at all periods the senate was full of "Stammerers" (*Balbi*), "Dolts" (*Bruti*), and so forth. But that is not to say these names were so many dead metaphors. In ordinary usage they were no doubt usually dormant, but they were always capable of being awakened to serve a purpose, including that of humorous invective. In this context it seems likely that Valerius names Afrania as wife of Senator Babbler in order to make the point that they are a matched pair. If the aristocratic Hortensia inherited her eloquence, then Afrania the arriviste married into a family of verbal ineptitude equal to her own.

It is rare that a woman is judged simply for her ability to speak or write rather than for her relationship to some man. Martial commends a contemporary poet, a certain Sulpicia, in a pair of epigrams that belong to a specific type, one in which a poet pays tribute to the work of an illustrious predecessor or an esteemed contemporary. Callimachus' epi-

[32] Hortensia is thought to have been married to Q. Servilius Caepio, who died in 67 BC, almost thirty years before Hortensia's speech. She is not known to have remarried, and the fact that she lived so long as a widow may explain why she, unlike Afrania, is remembered in connection with her famous father rather than her husband; but I believe Valerius is being very deliberate in his contrasting treatment of these women. See Hallett (1984), 58–59 (on Hortensia), 234 (on Afrania).

[33] Afrania's husband is the only Licinius Stolo listed by Broughton (1951–52), 2:493, who knows him only from this anecdote.

[34] *garrulus, quod ceteros oris loquacitate, non sensu exsuperat* (*Orig.* 10.1.30).

70

gram in honor of Aratus' *Phaenomena* (*Epigr.* 27 Pfeiffer) is a famous example; Catullus' witty distinction between the *Zmyrna* of his friend Cinna and the *Annales* of the detested Volusius is another (*Carm.* 95). Generally the poetry itself is the focus of these pieces, and the terms of praise indicate the literary ideals shared by both *laudator* and *laudandus*. An example from Martial's own day is Statius' poem on Lucan.[35] Statius praises Lucan in cosmic terms, comparing him with the greatest of his predecessors and citing specific poetic achievements, most notably of course his epic on the civil wars – so great an achievement, Statius says, that he was unwilling to expose himself to comparison by celebrating Lucan in hexameters.

In the light of this tradition, what is curious is that Martial praises Sulpicia while hardly mentioning her actual work. To be sure, her poems, as we hear in the first epigram (10.35), should be widely read. They are love poems full of play, charm, and wit. They suggest the pleasures that the Nymph Egeria shared with King Numa. But beyond such generalities, we get little specific impression of Sulpicia's writing. We hear that it does not deal with mythological disasters like Thyestes' banquet nor with scandalous heroines like Medea, Scylla, or Byblis. What we hear most about is Sulpicia herself: there was no one naughtier (*nequiorem* 11), but at the same time no one more proper (*sanctiorem* 12). If Sappho had studied with her she would have been not only *doctior*, but *pudica* as well (16); and if Sappho's hard-hearted lover, Phaon, had known them both, he would have fallen for Sulpicia (17–18). I note that there is no question of Phaon's reading their poetry: Martial evidently envisions a kind of beauty contest (N.B. *uisam* 17). Here he exploits the idea that Sappho was not beautiful and cleverly manipulates the ambivalent tradition concerning her sexuality. Had Sulpicia been a member of Sappho's *thiasos*, Sappho too would naturally have fallen in love with her, but learned to imitate her *pudicitia* – that is, Sulpicia would not have responded to Sappho's erotic advances, but would have taught Sappho to love men instead of girls. Or rather, not men but one man, for this is the dominant theme of the poem and the cornerstone of Martial's encomium: Sulpicia would have rejected Phaon's advances, as

---

[35] Statius' birthday poem for Lucan (*Siluae* 2.7), which was commissioned by the poet's widow, Polla Argentaria (*Siluae* 2, *pr.*), provides an instructive contrast with Martial's roughly contemporary epigrams on Sulpicia.

she would Jupiter's, Bacchus', or Apollo's, because her love for Calenus was deep and exclusive. This is what her poems teach, *castos ... et probos amores* (8), legitimate love between one man and one woman: this is the sense in which Sappho would have been *doctior* (16) for knowing Sulpicia, not as a better poet, but as a woman whose passions would have been channeled in the proper direction. Sulpicia is praised less as a poet of love than as a paragon of *uniuiratus* (2).

In Martial's second epigram (10.38) we lose sight of the poetry altogether: it is a poem of congratulations to Calenus on having such a wife. For we learn here that theirs was a married relationship, and not the uncommitted or even adulterous affair that was usual in Latin love poetry. It is true that these poems are written with a keen awareness of elegiac tradition and that they allude knowingly to Catullus and Propertius in particular. It is probable that they are following Sulpicia's own poetry in this regard, and that they allude to her work in ways that we cannot now recover.[36] But the one scrap of her verse that does survive suggests that Sulpicia could write in a way that challenged Martial at his most salacious and that he could not find adequate terms to praise. We can thank a late antique comment on the rare word *cadurcum* in Juvenal (6.537) for preserving what is probably our only authentic scrap of Sulpicia's poetry: "Probus says that the female part is to be understood, this being its covering; or, as others have it, a strap upon which a bed is laid, whence Sulpicia says: '... if [only?] when the bands of the bed-straps (*cadurci*) | have been restored, [it?] might display me to [or with?] Calenus, lying there naked....'"[37] This fragment does not disagree with anything Martial tells us, but it certainly adds to his rather coy remark that there is no one "naughtier" than Sulpicia. Seldom do we find anything either as explicit or as suggestive as this in the male elegists. To begin with, the poet's own body is hardly ever on view. Moreover, though the genre is notorious for teasing the reader with fleeting glimpses of the *puella* in half light or through Coan silks, when-

---

[36] Parker (1992), Hallett (1992), and Richlin (1992a) do an excellent job of situating Sulpicia in literary history.

[37] *membrum mulieris (inquit Probus) intellegitur, cum sit membri muliebris uelamen; uel, ut alii, est instita qua lectus intenditur, unde ait Sulpicia: "si me cadurci restitutis fasciis | nudam Caleno concubantem proferat."* For the text see Wessner (1931), 108.

ever the elegiac *amator* seems ready at last to train his gaze upon the ideal female form, he averts his eyes, and the reader's as well. Sulpicia is different: both poet and *puella*, she seizes the male prerogative of authorship and with it a gendered gaze which she trains upon her own body as she lies naked on a bed that has evidently been ruined once already by vigorous use. But she too manipulates the gaze by informing the reader either that she is not alone, but with Calenus, or else that her exhibitionism is intended solely for him. This is a very different sort of tease from the vicarious longing experienced through identification with the Propertian or Ovidian lover as he looks upon his *puella.* Nor do we often find this manipulation of the gaze enacted at the level of diction as well: the bed, its supporting bands restored (*fasciis restitutis*), has in effect put on one of the garments that Sulpicia has removed (the *fascia* being also a band used to support the breasts), even as the *double entendre* of *cadurcum* hints broadly not so much at the pleasure that Sulpicia intends for Calenus, but that she anticipates for herself. The boldness of this fragment makes Martial's praise look like simple prudishness even as it offers a hint of Latin erotic poetry in the feminine voice. It is as if Martial were spokesman for a culture that could not tolerate the idea of a woman writing as a poet of desire, both expressing her own and constructing an image of herself as the object of a man's *cupido*, without insisting that she was not so much a poet as she was the ideal Roman wife – not the voice and embodiment of physical passion such as we never encounter it in the Latin poetry written by men, but in the last analysis a traditional *uniuira* after all.

In AD 401, Torquatus Gennadius copied out a complete text of the works of Martial. His work produced one of the three families of manuscripts (and one of the two families that preserve unexpurgated texts) on which modern editions depend.[38] It was probably at this time that the works of classical authors were first being transferred from papyrus rolls to parchment codices. The decision whether a given work was worth the trouble determined whether it would survive into the Middle Ages. Gennadius chose to copy Martial for posterity; what did he decide to leave behind? Let us imagine that Gennadius had made a rather specific choice. Suppose that he had before him one *capsa* containing the epigrams of Martial and another with the love poems of

---

[38] For details and further references see Reeve (1983).

Sulpicia Caleni. Suppose he had decided, instead of writing out Martial's works, to copy Sulpicia's. What else would have been different, if it had happened this way? What would have had to be different in order to make this happen? What might it be like to live in a world accustomed to hearing Latin spoken in a powerful female voice?

The sisters of Vibia Perpetua

The Roman woman never fully escapes from her relationship to at least one man. Always, it seems, there is either son, or father, or husband, and perhaps all of these. The male writer may write to and for other men without ever mentioning women; the opposite almost never occurs. To illustrate this point, let us return one last time to Valerius Maximus' chapter on lady orators. I have discussed his second and third examples, Afrania and Hortensia, the former characterized as her husband's wife, the latter as her father's daughter. Only the first example in this series does not present the woman speaker as a dependent of some man. Maesia Sentinas, Valerius observes, spoke in her own defense in a celebrated case of unknown date and was not only acquitted, but acquitted almost unanimously. Beyond this essential information Valerius is tantalizingly vague about the entire incident. What was the charge that Maesia faced? Why did she not entrust her defense to experienced advocates? Does a reference to haste on the part of the presiding magistrate (*L. Titio praetore iudicium cogente*) suggest that the case was rushed to trial and that she was given inadequate time to make the usual preparations, even to secure adequate counsel? However this may be, Valerius certainly gives Maesia credit for conducting her defense "not just capably, but bravely" in every respect.[39] Equally relevant is the fact that she is endowed with no male relatives, cognate or agnate. This may explain in part why she must speak in her own defense, but it also seemingly deprives Valerius of the opportunity to explain her exploit with reference to those of some man. As her story develops, however, we see that this is precisely the point that he wants to make. According to his lights, the style of any lady orator like Hortensia or an orataster like Afrania must be represented even if only tacitly in terms of her relationship to

---

[39] *non solum diligenter, sed etiam fortiter* (8.3.1).

some man. But in Maesia's case there is no man. The obvious inference must be the one that the story draws, namely that beneath her feminine appearance lurks a man's heart, that she is herself, in some sense, male. And this is in fact the case; after her great victory, "because she bore a man's courage beneath a lady's looks, people began calling her 'the Androgyne'."[40]

The matter of nomenclature again is critical. Because she has no husband or father, Valerius introduces his subject merely as Maesia Sentinas. Her nomen is the Sabellian equivalent of Maia, and her cognomen suggests that she is from the mountain town of Sentinum. She is thus marked with a name that, even if Roman, is not quite Latin. After prevailing in court, moreover, she was no longer known as Maesia Sentinas, but as Maesia Androgyne, a new name that moves her even farther away from the center of Latin culture beyond the pale of Sabellian territory into the realm of linguistic otherness that is Greece. Maesia's story thus belongs not only to the class represented in this chapter, stories about women at the bar, but equally to etiological tales like those about Valerius Corvinus and Manlius Torquatus that explain the origins of their *cognomina*. But normally such stories are told about old war heroes; Maesia's is one of the very few we have that is told about a woman. Her androgynous title thus becomes doubly appropriate: she is a transgressive figure both in her behavior before the tribunal and in the unusual name that her achievement earns.

In Maesia's new name we find an ancient analogue to modern theoretical speculations concerning the sex of the elder Sulpicia. When a woman speaks Latin her utterance must be traced to some masculine subject, even if that subject is a presumptive aspect of character or personality that lurks within herself, giving the lie to her feminine appearance. Throughout most of antiquity the woman who speaks or writes in Latin is suspected of harboring an inappropriately masculine nature, and this suspicion itself becomes grounds for disapproving of and suppressing her voice.

Not until what is now called late antiquity do we find the beginnings of a change. It is at this point that we encounter the most important

---

[40] *Quam, quia sub specie feminae uirilem animum gerebat, "Androgynen" appellabat* (8.3.1).

surviving voice of feminine latinity in the writings of an early Christian martyr named Vibia Perpetua.[41] This woman has been hailed with justice as one of the most original voices not only of latinity but of all world literature. Perpetua left a kind of diary describing her arrest and the events leading up to her martyrdom in the amphitheater of Roman Carthage on March 7, AD 203. Her narrative is accompanied by that of a fellow martyr named Saturus, and both of these narratives are supplemented and bound together by still another, anonymous frame that provides an introduction and conclusion to the entire event. The various accounts are thus preserved as a single composite document; the voices of the different writers are distinguished partly by their varying perspectives in the events of which they tell, but mainly by their individual, very distinctive, styles.

Perpetua's own narrative is by far the most striking portion of the text. Unlike the framing narrative, which is rhetorically ambitious in a way that quickly becomes wearying and obtrusive, or the connecting narrative, which is plain and undistinguished, Perpetua's account strikes every reader as simple and direct, vibrant in its images, frank and unembarrassed. While Perpetua is usually hailed for being the first woman writer of antiquity to leave an account of her own life and experiences, she is important in several other respects as well. Her experiences themselves – her arrest and martyrdom, her break with her family, and so on – are remarkable and vividly related. Her narrative contains accounts of her astounding dreams, dreams that are more distinctive and detailed, more dreamlike, in fact, than any others we know from the ancient world. Her testimony is one of our earliest documents of Christian Latin as well, full of usages that have been identified as marking a distinctive idiolect. For our purposes, an additional element deserves mention. Perpetua's narrative is full of men. Her father, her son, her brother, her husband, her judges and executioners, figures who appear in her dreams, all are men. So her narrative is surrounded by men, or so we think: the authors of the connecting and framing narrative are at least assumed to be men, and certainly we know that the male power structure of the early North African Church was at pains to

---

[41] Essential reading: Dronke (1984), 1–17; Shaw (1993). Habermehl (1992) gives a good literary analysis; Nolan (1994) considers Perpetua as exemplifying a "feminine poetics of revelation."

interpret Perpetua's words in productive ways that would contain and control the enthusiasm that her experiences generated within the Christian community. In this respect, Perpetua is very much like the earlier heroines of feminine latinity whom we have been discussing, Cornelia, Hortensia, the two Sulpicias. The structure of the work in which her story reaches us in fact resembles the transmission of the elder Sulpicia's poetry in several crucial ways. In the case of Sulpicia, gender suspicion is both an artifact of the manuscript tradition that transmits her poetry as the work of Tibullus, and a discursive problem that arises from the difficulty of situating this lone female authorial voice within the otherwise exclusively if anxiously masculine tradition of Roman elegiac poetry. In this respect Sulpicia's elegies resemble Perpetua's diary, each being examples of a woman's writing handed down by men in the context of notably masculinist social and literary institutions complete with a (presumably) male-authored literary frame that comments upon the woman writer's *ipsissima uerba*. The theme of the writer's uncertain gender is however only barely suggested by Sulpicia's poetry. In Perpetua's case the story is very different.

In the first place, Sulpicia is very conventional in positioning herself *vis à vis* the various men in her life. Messalla plays the role of benevolent uncle, Cerinthus that of youthful (and irresponsible) lover. When Sulpicia's pride is wounded she styles herself as her father's daughter by her full, aristocratic Roman name, *Serui filia Sulpicia*.[42] But where Sulpicia is conventional, Perpetua is revolutionary. She opens her narrative with an account of how she rejected her father by insisting that she was a Christian. Her behavior provokes him to violence – he makes as if to scratch her eyes out – and she tells how relieved she was to be rid of him for a few days. A major theme of the ensuing narrative is Perpetua's casting off of her male relatives, all those who represent some sort of cultural obligation. She has a baby son, for whom she shows tender concern, until she suddenly decides he does not need her anymore, and leaves him to her father. We have no idea who the boy's father may be. Only her brother, Dinocrates, matters to her – not because he is her brother; he had died, evidently some time ago, at the age of seven, and after that "never entered my mind." But she spontaneously speaks his

---

[42] [Tibullus] 3.16/4.10.4; cf. Valerius Maximus' treatment of Hortensia, discussed above.

name while praying, and then he appears to her in dreams. First he is tormented like Tantalus, standing thirsty in a pool of water from which he cannot drink; then, after she prays for him, she sees the boy drinking his fill from the same pool. After this vision, Perpetua's father visits her in prison, and the contrast is extreme: she pities him, but can do nothing for him.

In addition to abrogating the role of the proper Roman woman towards these various men, Perpetua actually becomes a kind of Maesia Androgyne. In her final vision, she sees herself in the arena where she is to die, facing an enormous Egyptian gladiator: "and I was stripped" (as a woman in the arena would be) "and became male."[43] As a male, she defeats the Egyptian in combat; and waking from her vision, she goes carefree to her death, knowing that she will be victorious in her struggle against the Enemy.

Perpetua's diary exists in both Latin and Greek versions. The overwhelming evidence that the Latin version is the original was once doubted because in this work we have at last an extended account of complex events possessing important public and private dimensions narrated in the female voice. It was once doubted that such a thing could occur in Latin. It is therefore crucial to remember how much of the work that has been done on Perpetua's writing stresses her substandard latinity. If her work was not actually composed in Greek, the argument seems to go, neither is it quite acceptable as Latin. It is in fact often adduced as a specimen of "Vulgar" or "Christian" Latin, sometimes of "African" Latin, or even of some other outlandish variety that does not pass muster by classical standards. Perhaps this is why classicists as a rule take so little interest in authors like Perpetua. Perhaps it is not her Christian latinity, but her Christian belief that is to blame. But neither reason is very compelling. Strict adherence over centuries to a narrow spectrum of approved stylistic possibilities is one of the most important factors that has winnowed the rich literary output of antiquity down to the (numerically) impoverished selection of authors that have actually survived. For classicists to acquiesce in and even contribute to maintaining this restrictive construction of latinity by neglecting authors as fascinating and important as Perpetua, either on stylistic or on ideological grounds, seems to me an act of intellectual

---

[43] *et expoliata sum et facta sum masculus* (10.7).

self-abnegation of which few other disciplines would be capable. Others may find this form of asceticism praiseworthy, but those that do should perhaps ask themselves exactly what is being gained by it and what is being lost.

In any case, Perpetua's diary stands as a foundational document of church history, of medieval literature, and of feminine latinity as well. Indeed, the three spheres can hardly be separated. From the perspective of Latin culture, the social and cultural changes that brought about the christianization of the empire are intimately and necessarily linked to the forces that drove both the "debasement" of classical Latin and the "rise" of vernacular speech – and allowed for the production and the preservation of significant bodies of writing by women. To be sure, cultural misogyny neither begins nor ends with the classical period of Latin culture; but just as that culture claims the masculine gender relative to Greece, so does it relegate the Middle Ages, religiously different and linguistically corrupt, to the role of the feminine. And just as Sappho stands as the eldest sister among the women poets of Greece, Perpetua too inaugurates a series of important female writers in the Latin Middle Ages: Egeria, Proba, Dhuoda, Hrotswitha of Gandersheim, the young women of Le Ronceray, Hildegard of Bingen, Heloise, and others. It is true that these women, widely separated by time and place, wrote very differently from one another, and that their combined oeuvre is dwarfed by the colossal literary output of medieval men. Unlike the women of the classical period, however, their work does survive. And despite the different conditions under which they lived, these medieval women share something with their more ancient counterparts: witness the aforementioned formal congruencies between Sulpicia's and Perpetua's writings; witness Dhuoda's *liber manualis* to her son William, like Cornelia's letters to Gaius an example of the "mirror of princes" genre, normally a bastion of masculinist literary prerogative, written by a father to his son. These later texts can do much to illuminate the earlier ones, and even to help us recover some sense of what has been lost.

What might it be like to live in a world accustomed to hearing Latin spoken in a powerful female voice? Perhaps this world is not beyond imagining; perhaps it even existed. In my previous chapter I mentioned the Duchess Hadwig, who lived during the tenth century at Castle Hohentwiel in Swabia, renowned for her beauty and her learning.

According to legend, the duchess was paid a visit by Ekkehard II, who brought along with him a young student named Purchart. Hadwig asked why the boy had come along. "On account of Greek, my lady," said Ekkehard. "I have brought the boy, who already knows much else, so that he might catch something from your mouth." With this the boy addressed the duchess himself, speaking in Latin hexameters:

> Esse uelim Grecus, cum uix sim, domna, Latinus.

> I would like to be a Greek, my lady, although I am scarcely a Latin.

Hadwig, delighted, drew the boy to her, kissed him, and asked him to continue speaking in verses. Purchart, "as if unaccustomed to such a kiss," replied:

> Non possum prorsus dignos componere uersus;
> nam nimis expaui, Duce me libante suaui.

> I cannot compose worthy verses straight away,
> for I was too startled when the Duchess gave me a sweet kiss.

This performance was a great success. This time Hadwig rewarded Purchart with a bit of Greek, an antiphon (*Maria et flumina*) that she had translated from the Latin:

> *Thalassi ke potami, eulogoi ton kyrion;*
> *Ymnite pigon ton kyrion alleluja.*

> Seas and rivers, praise the Lord; fountains, sing alleluia to the Lord.

The boy became a great favorite, remaining for some time at Hadwig's court, chattering to her in his impromptu hexameters and learning Greek from her; and when he left, she also presented him with a Horace and several other books "which," the author of this anecdote informs us, "our library [of St. Gall] contains today."[44]

Associations of gender and language run all through this tale as do the themes of wealth and poverty, coming of age, power and learning, the sacred and the profane. Let us begin with the fact that at the story's center stands Hadwig, a woman of wealth, power, beauty, and formi-

---

[44] Ekkehard, *Casus S. Galli* 94, ed. Haefele (1980), 194.

dable learning. From this woman Purchart, the aspiring Greek scholar, hopes to gain some instruction, "to have something from her lips." Something of this *double entendre* is already present in a detail that we learn elsewhere, that Hadwig herself learned Greek from a eunuch. Is language instruction such an intimate exchange that precautions must be taken against more physical forms of intercourse? Or is Greek itself figured here as a language expressly suited to seduction? In any case, when the duchess does grant Purchart's request, she does not follow up the kiss with love poetry, but instead teaches him a hymn that she is supposed to have translated from the Latin and, eventually, presents him with a volume of pagan wisdom as well.

Hadwig is a remarkable and imposing figure, one in whom power, position, and classical learning are linked to one another – in itself, of course, an unremarkable collocation – and, more importantly, to a frank female sexuality that is not incompatible with conventional piety. The image of learning in Latin or in Greek that Hadwig presents is certainly not paternal, nor yet maternal, but involves other aspects of the feminine than classical thought can comfortably acknowledge. Such a woman was no doubt remarkable even in her own time. In an earlier age, she would have been an abomination. Not that such did not exist; perhaps they existed in great plenty. But those few of whom we know, women comfortable with power, formidable in their learning, and liberated in their sexuality, were never portrayed as this story presents the duchess. A more typical example would be the notorious Sempronia, a noblewoman involved in the Catilinarian conspiracy, of whom Sallust has left a memorable sketch.[45] We know of Sempronia only what Sallust tells us in his remarkable and gratuitous excursus. She is little more to us than a bit of rhetorical color fashioned expressly to serve the historian's moralizing purposes. But she is instructive. In particular, she has a lot in common with Duchess Hadwig, who lived a thousand years after her. Both women were favored with high birth, personal beauty, intelligence, wit, the best education, and excellent connections. In Hadwig's case, these qualities supported her high position, which in turn gave her the freedom to use and enjoy all of her considerable talents to the fullest extent. Sempronia, too, according to Sallust,

[45] Sallust, *Cat.* 25.

enjoyed herself; but in so doing she not only ruined her finances and reputation, but became involved in a disastrous revolutionary plot.[46]

The masculine culture of the Roman period works always to coopt and to occlude the feminine, which nevertheless threatens constantly to return, to expose the masculine as a construction, as a pose. This threat surfaces most clearly in the discourse on linguistic effeminacy. At all times faulty speech could be equated with deviant sexuality. The elder Seneca, writing to his sons, rails against the softness of their contemporaries who are incapable of the labor it would take to perfect their speech: "Who of your age is – why say 'clever enough', 'diligent enough'? No; who is *man* enough?"[47] Centuries later Alan of Lille would equate sexual with grammatical passivity:

Actiui generis sexus se turpiter horret
   sic in passiuum degenerare genus.
Femina uir factus sexus denigrat honorem,
   ars magice Veneris hermafroditat eum.
Praedicat et subicit, fit duplex terminus idem,
   grammatice leges ampliat ille nimis.
Se negat esse uirum Nature, factus in arte
   barbarus. Ars illi non placet, immo tropus.
Non tamen ista tropus poterit translatio dici,
   in uicium melius ista figura cadit.

The active sex shudders in disgrace as it sees itself degenerate into the passive sex. A man turned into a woman blackens the fair name of his sex. The witchcraft of Venus turns him into a hermaphrodite. He is subject and predicate: one and the same term is given a double application. Man extends here too far the laws of grammar. Becoming a barbarian in grammar, he disclaims the manhood given him by nature. Grammar does not find favor with him but rather a trope. This transposition, however, cannot be called a trope. The figure here falls more directly into the category of defects.[48]

---

[46] On this general theme see Richlin (1992b).

[47] *Quis aequalium uestrorum quid dicam satis ingeniosus, satis studiosus, immo quis satis uir est?* (*Con.* 1 pr. 9).

[48] *De planctu Naturae* metr. 1, tr. Ziolkowski (1985). The Latin text is ed. Häring (1978), 806–07.

This passage introduces a central theme of the *Complaint of Nature*, which will later condemn same-sex unions as "solecisms" and recommend only the active voice of transitive verbs as a proper model for human conjugation, deploring intransitives, reflexives, passives, and especially deponents as patterns of deviant sexual practices.[49] "Masculine" speech then possesses certain characteristics that Latin culture universally admires, traits that even women can assimilate. By the same token, the "natural" faults of "feminine" speech also appear in the language of deficient men – men whose speech is untutored, rustic, excessively old-fashioned, or otherwise beyond the linguistic pale. In some cases men speak in a way that can only be characterized as effeminate: this would mean that they lisp or mumble, swallow syllables or endings, fail to modulate their voices in a manly way. These faults may be symptoms of poor training or of inferior natural capacity. All, I would note, are congruent with the kinds of linguistic changes that occurred as Latin gave rise to Romance.

In Latin culture women play the role of the linguistic Other. At best they may attain to a nearly masculine linguistic culture. The most successful can almost pass as men, particularly in the eyes of modern readers; the most admired betray no quality of their own, but rather embody the masculine latinity of their fathers and more distant male ancestors. More typically, women represent an inferior and degenerate latinity that correlates with various substandard types: socially with plebeian, spatially with provincial, religiously with Christian, chronologically with medieval and vernacular speech. The project of recovering the feminine voice of latinity is as fascinating in itself as it is essential to the intellectual health of Latin studies. But the practical and theoretical problems that it involves will not allow that project to succeed if it does not extend itself beyond the limits of classical antiquity.

---

[49] *De planctu Naturae* pr. 4, 5. On this topic see Ziolkowski (1985).

The life cycle of dead languages

Structures of literary and cultural history

My previous chapter runs counter to the main argument of this book in one important respect. I want to maintain that Latin culture is best and most fully represented by the Latin language itself, and that it should be seen as a larger and more unified area than traditional disciplinary structures currently allow. But by accepting even provisionally the idea that classical Latin is gendered masculine, and medieval Latin feminine, or by locating medieval Latin in an intermediate zone of ambiguous gender between masculine, classical speech and the feminine vernacular, I am implicitly endorsing one of the longest-lived distinctions, and argu-ably the most pernicious, ever imposed upon latinity from ancient times down to the present.

Of course, Latin culture is vast and various. Even though we must try to comprehend it as a whole, it would be impossible to do so without some sense of interior articulation, whether by chronological periods, regional traditions, or other organizing principles. Problems occur when structures that arose to facilitate one kind of understanding end up blocking other channels of communication. This has unquestionably happened in the case of the most prevalent histories of Latin culture.

A recent book asks whether it is still possible to write literary his-tory.[1] Some might further question whether it is even desirable. But for students of a phenomenon as long-lived as Latin culture, historical thinking is indispensable, and the institutionalized maps and taxon-

---

[1] Perkins (1992).

omies of previous generations are almost impossible to do without. Further, concepts such as "classical antiquity" and "the Middle Ages" belong to a much larger intellectual construct than that of latinity alone; the conflicting valences of continuity and periodization beset all forms of historical discourse. The strength of formal history is its ability to incorporate an enormous amount of specific detail and easily to account for relationships among parallel time lines, subsidiary movements, and all manner of related structures. It is also true that these structures eventually harden and become the kind of intellectual compartments into which a scholar might pour the professional energy of an entire career. It may be easy to assert that "the Augustan period" and "late antiquity" are merely convenient talking points that enable one sort of discussion and are not meant to preclude the possibility of others. But when a discipline becomes populated mainly by specialists in areas like "the Augustan period" or "late antiquity," and when initiates view the process of acculturation largely as a matter of acquiring professional competence in only one such area, the devices that we use to organize that discipline quickly begin to look less like temporary room dividers that might be easily moved around from day to day as the ongoing discussion requires, and more like mountain ranges that one could spend a lifetime either climbing over or going around – if one did not die of exposure in the attempt.

A critique of periodization must begin by historicizing the notion of periodization itself. I will not attempt a complete history of literary history even in the realm of Latin alone. It will be useful, however, to consider some of the structures that have been imposed on Latin culture in order to understand better the metaphors one uses when speaking and thinking about it.

Linguistic miscegenation

Historians of latinity tend to be obsessed with decline. It can be argued that these historians are simply following the lead of ancient authorities – the elder Seneca, for instance, and most notably Tacitus. These spokesmen for the debasement of latinity appear at first sight to validate modern chroniclers of linguistic and cultural entropy. But to make this judgment involves an important oversight. Our ancient and, for that matter, medieval historians of debased latinity are indeed concerned with the problem of decadence. What they do not do is adopt an objectively judgmental perspective on a literary–historical version of the "absolute past"; rather they discuss the conditions under which they see themselves as having to live. It is not possible for the modern historian naively to endorse as fact an argument by any ancient or medieval predecessor about the decline of Latin culture. Each witness has his own axe to grind, and uses the motif of decline to serve different and highly contingent purposes. Tacitus, for example, is concerned with the demise of senatorial prerogative under the principate; bemoaning the loss under earlier emperors of *libertas* – free speech for the aristocracy – sets off his praise for the enlightened policies of Trajan, Tacitus' imperial patron. In any case, if one judges simply as a connoisseur of latinity itself, the conditions that produced such a master as Tacitus can hardly be regretted, nor does it make much sense to view these conditions as characteristic of an enervated age.

In another important perspective on decline, Isidore of Seville compares the excellence of Latin with that of Greek. He clearly imagines the Greek and Latin languages in quite different ways even at points when they seem by his own logic to resemble one another closely. Greek, he tells us, has five dialects. Of these, Koine is spoken everywhere, Attic is associated with Athens, Doric (curiously) with Egypt and Syria, Ionic and Aeolic (presumably; here he does not specify, and the text is slightly uncertain) with Ionia and Aeolia, respectively. Linguistic diversity is therefore mainly a function of geographical dispersion. Not entirely, however: Attic is said to enjoy a special status as the dialect "that all the Greek authors used" (*qua usi sunt omnes Graeciae auctores*). This is wrong, of course. Ionic, Doric, and Aeolic were literary as well as spoken dialects. Note, however, that the spatial dispersion of Attic is matched by that of Koine, "the mixed or common language that everyone uses" (*mixta siue communis quam omnes utuntur*). Indeed, the very order in which Isidore lists these dialects gives primacy to Koine as the medium of exchange among all Greek speakers and to Attic as the literary language of all Greek authors. There is in addition some consciousness that while Attic, the prestige dialect of *belles-lettres*, is the language of one city, Koine is uniquely important because it is used all over the Greek world. Within this predominantly spatial arrangement, then, Isidore presents the Greek language largely as a synchronic artifact existing in various forms and in various places at all times in both panhellenic (Koine and, in literature, Attic) and epichoric (Doric, Ionic, and Aeolic) manifestations. Greek culture is thus organized by symmetrical relationships between space and language that have obtained from the very beginning.[2] Finally, note that Isidore says nothing explicitly about the penetration of the language into alien space (as he might have done, since he places Doric in Egypt and Syria) or about its development in other ways over time.

Isidore's perspective on the diversity of Latin speech shares certain features with, and in some sense probably derives from, his account of Greek (which is in turn largely traditional).[3] There is, for example, a dialect that resembles Koine in that it is said to be "mixed," and again mixing is related to spatial extension. But in contrast to the situation of Greek, the spatial extension of Latin culture is a gradual process that correlates with development over time. Moreover, this mixing involves the contamination of the native language by alien influences imported from without as the inevitable concomitant of political and territorial expansion. "Mixed [latinity] invaded the Roman state along with foreign peoples and their customs after the boundaries of the empire had expanded considerably, corrupting the integrity of the language with solecisms and barbarisms."[4] Isidore associates latinity with Italy, especially with Latium and, of course, Rome. He views the growth of the empire, in sharp contrast to Gibbon, not as a process of taking civilized speech to the rest of the world, but rather as the mechanism by which

---

[2] Versteegh (1987). Koine, the synthetic dialect, is not impure Greek, but is to be understood either as an amalgam of the various regional dialects presumably developed to cope with the diversity of Greek speech in different parts of the world or even – and surprisingly to us – as the original and most correct form of Greek.

[3] A five-part division of Greek illustrates the linguistic mastery of Crassus the "triumvir" (Quintilian *IO* 11.2.50, Val. Max. 8.7.6), but this tradition does not specify what "parts," whether dialects or not, are at issue. There exists an alternate tradition dividing the Greek language into four dialects, and it seems possible that this structure underlies Isidore's four-part division of Latin. I am grateful to Professor Anna Morpurgo Davies for discussion of these points.

[4] *Mixta, quae post imperium latius promotum simul cum moribus et hominibus in Romanam ciuitatem inrumpit, integritatem uerbi per soloecismos et barbarismos corrumpens* (*Orig.* 9.1.7). On "solecism" and "barbarism" see my discussion in ch. 2.

latinity is corrupted to the point of barbarization. The Mixed dialect of Latin is clearly an inferior version, tainted in a way that (in Isidore's terms) Koine is not.

One might have viewed the history of the Greek language in a similar light. Generally, however, Greek culture even as it endured a lengthy period of political imbecility has been seen as asserting its intellectual and even linguistic hegemony over Rome. While Latin culture was, *à la* Gibbon, imposing its civilizing influence on barbarian peoples, barbarian speech was (in the western provinces) already undermining the linguistic purity of the newly received Latin culture; while, in the east, an uncontaminated Greek culture remained proof against Latin influence. Greek in fact gained ground among the Roman intelligentsia even within the capital. Whatever damage was inflicted upon the Greeks by the export of their culture throughout the Mediterranean world did not prevent a new cultural ascendency during the *pax Romana* as latinity, debilitated by conquest, passed the apex of its perfection and experienced a steep decline on all sides.

Viewed from such a perspective, Isidore's history of Latin agrees perfectly with modern narratives of cultural recession. But Isidore stands apart from later chroniclers of decline in one important respect: he clearly implicates himself within his pattern. His own use in this passage of *utor* with the accusative as well as the ablative attests that he is a creature of this postlapsarian world. But one cannot help being impressed by the fact that Isidore ties the beginning of linguistic decadence to the appearance of the Roman empire itself. The latest authors he cites from the great period before the decline are Cicero, the last great orator of the free Republic, and Virgil, the poet who heralded Augustus' foundation of world empire. The force that Isidore holds to account for linguistic decadence differs from the one on which Tacitus had blamed the decline of public eloquence; but the periodization of Latin culture that results from these two perceptions of decline is very much the same.

Though Isidore, too, charts the decline of latinity over time, his response to decline is healthier and more productive than many that would follow. Like Tacitus, he deserves credit for simply getting on with it: despite his rueful perspective on the cultural tendencies of his own time, he never descended to a condition of paralysis or aporia. He not only resists despair, but sets an example for coping with reduced circumstances. Isidore's account of Latin dialects forms part of a discussion about the metaphysical importance of the *tres linguae sacrae*, Hebrew, Greek, and Latin – the languages of the inscription that was fixed to the Savior's cross. Within such a context, it is clear that the political and demographic conditions that developed under the Roman empire are reinscribed within a biblical narrative – specifically, the crucially important myth of the Tower of Babel. The decline of latinity from acmaic perfection to barbarous heteroglossia thus recapitulates the linguistic history of humankind as a whole. From this perspective, Isidore appears not as an advocate of retrenchment or of shrinking expectations, but as one of the most formative intellectual forces in Europe over the subsequent seven or eight centuries.

For this reason it is worth taking Isidore's model of linguistic and cultural history at least as seriously as other models that have informed the disciplinary structure of Latin studies. Isidore's conception of a mixed and developing latinity is a powerful counterforce to Dante's sharp dichotomy between stable grammatical speech and a vernacular that is in hopeless flux.[5] Where Dante's Latin is incapable of change, Isidore speaks of four distinct periods; nor does he identify change exclusively with decline. The Latin of Isidore's first period is called *Prisca*, a word that never means merely "old" but which always bears connotations of a perfect, uncorrupted, originary state.[6] But Isidore hardly suggests that this was the Latin language's finest hour. On the contrary, he regards its remains as "uncouth" (*incondita*) and from what we know of the genre he adduces in illustration – the priestly hymns of the state religion that superstitious conservatism accurately preserved in an unintelligible condition – his assessment is understandable. This period gave way to the "Latin" period, which if we judge by its name might have witnessed the ideal condition of the Latin language. It is of course notable – and ironic in view of Isidore's later assessment of foreign influence on the language – that the Latin period coincides with the domination of Rome by Etruscan kings. This is the

---

[5] See my discussion in ch. 1.

[6] Isidore defines the Pristine dialect as the one spoken under the reign of Saturn, i.e. during the Golden Age of pagan mythology.

period of the Twelve Tables, which also survive in part, and by comparing the remains to those of the priestly hymns sung when gods ruled on earth we can measure the progress of Latin speech under human kings from superstitious babble to legal precept. But it is clearly the third or Roman period when the language reached its apex under a republican form of government (*post reges exactos a populo Romano*) and, in the hands of men worthy to be called "poets" and "orators," became a literary medium. Only when the republican government of the *populus Romanus* is overwhelmed by the imperial state does linguistic decline set in; and Isidore, writing in the sixth century from one of the former provinces of that empire, sees no reason religious, political, or otherwise to distinguish the Mixed period that clearly began in earlier antiquity from the time in which he lives or from any time that is to follow.

Isidore does not speculate on the future of Latin culture. The model that he proposes, however, clearly conforms to an acmaic model, one that imagines a not quite undifferentiated but sparsely attested period of building towards a consummation or perfection that cannot last. The chief emphasis of all such models involves a defining contrast between the brief classical moment and the vast stretch of inferior time that follows. But unlike other models of decline, this one did not work merely to focus attention on a single period of imaginary perfection in the immediate or distant past. Instead, it served as an aetion for the conditions of polymorphous latinity that prevailed over the next eight hundred years. In this respect, Isidore's concept of mixed latinity stands in sharp contrast to prevailing models of cultural history that have informed Latin studies for generations and that have militated against the formation of a more holistic and unified perspective of Latin culture in its entirety.

Gold and silver, bronze and iron

After the distinction between classical and medieval Latin, the most widespread, not to say hackneyed trope of Latin literary history is without question the quasi-Hesiodic "myth of ages." Latin literature has long been divided into two central periods of paramount importance, one "gold" and the other "silver." These labels are much less popular than they once were, but their influence remains despite efforts in recent years to reimagine the distinction in other terms.[7] In fact, most of these efforts have accepted the existing structure more or less implicitly, but have attempted to remove the judgmental connotations of the received imagery by substituting words like "early imperial" for "silver." This isn't really much of a change. Rather like BCE and CE for BC and AD, it actually endorses the traditional structure of history while proposing new, more "politically correct" labels for the very same historical periods. The new labels tend to occlude some of the further prejudicial elements latent within the "Hesiodic" model, just as BCE and CE coyly skirt the issue of the singular event that divides the epochs that they name; but as I have suggested above, more progress is to be made by aggressively exposing and analyzing these unspoken elements than by sweeping them under the carpet or recycling them in superficially more palatable terms.

The appeal of this imagery consists partly, no doubt, in the fact that it explains Latin cultural history in terms of Greek myth. In addition to this, it is always comforting, as I noted above, to base ideas about the ancient world on the explicit statements of ancient witnesses, no matter how interested or tendentious their testimony may be; and by adopting this particular trope, the modern historian is following in the footsteps of no less an authority than Virgil, who virtually claimed to preside over a cultural golden age. So strong is the appeal of this imagery that it has frequently been applied to the history of Latin literature despite the fact that (unlike Isidore's model) it leaves the entire period prior to the first century BC entirely out of account. But the most notable feature of this literary–historical "myth of ages" is that it is regularly edited so as to remove the later stages of decadence, bronze and iron – to say nothing of Hesiod's problematic race of heroes, swimming against a steady tide of decline. Clearly an idiom that speaks only of "gold" and "silver" both hypostasizes the idea of decline within the classical period (again unlike Isidore's model) and casts an even more pejorative light on whatever follows. Further, the fact that what follows is usually not discussed as part of this scheme suggests clearly enough that the supposititious

---

[7] Students of what has traditionally been called "the silver age" tend to complain about the designation (e.g. Boyle [1988], 1), but have not yet managed to invent another that has gained widespread acceptance. Metallic vocabulary is still used without apology in Kenney and Clausen (1982), 497–98 and Conte (1994), 406.

periods of bronze and iron are simply not interesting to an audience concerned with the history of Latin literature. Thus the biometallic model not only reinforces the aforementioned division between classical and medieval Latin; as it is commonly used, it simply elides the great gulf of history that separates antiquity from the modern world.

This raises again the issue of perspective. Like Isidore's system, the "myth of ages" clearly presupposes the eventual decline of Latin culture. Unlike Isidore's system, it does not carry out the implications of its imagery to the end. Do modern latinists have a place in this system, or do we stand entirely outside it? The latter, apparently: I have yet to find a modern historian of Latin literature moaning like Hesiod about living in an age of iron. In fact, those who take a view like the one implied in this biometallic model implicitly claim a privileged perspective with respect to the entire history of Latin culture – a position from which they are able to see that culture whole, to know it, and judge it objectively. How did they come to find themselves in this enviable position?

Philology recapitulates ontology

By referring to the "*bio*metallic" model I am not alluding simply to Hesiod's myth of gold and silver "races." The "myth of ages" has for much of the modern period been read as part of a larger pattern that involves modelling the history of latinity on the life cycle of higher organisms. The preferred exemplar is, of course, the human species. No metaphor packs quite so much intuitive conviction or perceived explanatory power as the biological fallacy. Sometimes couched in terms of "rise and fall" that (barely) conceal their origins, such models frequently elaborate the biological sources of their symbolic language to the point of self-deconstruction.

An exemplary version of this system, and surely the most developed specimen, is that of Johann Nicolaus Funck, an eighteenth-century philologist and literary historian.[8] Between 1720 and 1750, Funck pub-

---

[8] The metaphor is certainly older than Funck, however. Scaliger (1561), 295 actually denies the validity of both the myth of ages and the human life cycle for understanding literary history, thereby suggesting that both models were in use by his time. Both systems are known to and used by Borrichius (1675), 1–2, who discusses the use of each by other scholars.

lished (*inter alia*) a series of works tracing the history of Latin from its origins to Carolingian times. The structure of his project relies explicitly on the biological fallacy to a truly humorous degree. The titles of the work's seven parts parade the author's faith in the exegetical power of metaphor. The individual parts deal with the "origin" of the Latin language: with its "boyhood," "adolescence," and "manhood;" with its "imminent," "still vigorous," and finally "inert and decrepit old age."[9] Nor is the allegory (as Funck himself styles it) a mere decorative touch intended to enliven a technical subject: on the contrary, Funck alludes to and defends this developmental model at a number of points throughout the seven treatises. In addition, he explicitly adopts the language of the "myth of ages," designating the *uirilis aetas* of the Latin language as a truly "golden age."[10]

It would be easy to dismiss Funck and his system as an amusing aberration in the history of scholarship, especially since no one reads him anymore. But by mixing his metaphors in this way, Funck elaborated a view of Latin literary and linguistic history that has become almost canonical. If we consult subsequent works, we immediately notice clear traces of the same logic (or, better, myth) that informs Funck's work. Indeed, Schanz and Hosius, in their standard history of Latin literature, praise Funck precisely for his attempt to distinguish the various periods of latinity in these terms.[11]

Carried out to the end, of course, the biological fallacy leads inevitably to the concept of "dead languages." Funck makes this point explicit in his seventh part, which deals with the *extrema ... eius linguae calamitas*, a period that begins with the sack of Rome in AD 410 and concludes with the death of Charlemagne, "together with whom latinity itself seems utterly to have perished" (*quocum ipsa latinitas penitus interiisse uidetur*). Why did the historian choose this terminus?

The structure of Funck's work suggests that he had said all he wanted to say about the history of Latin culture, perhaps even all that could be

---

[9] Funccius (1720–50). The Latin titles of the individual parts are: (1) *De origine Latinae linguae*, (2) *De pueritia*, (3) *De adolescentia*, (4) *De uirili aetate*, (5) *De imminenti*, (6) *De uegeta*, (7) *De inerti ac decrepita Latinae linguae senectute*.

[10] Funccius (1720–50), 3:2. True to form, he develops the metallic motif to include not only gold, silver, bronze, and iron, but lead as well (Funccius (1750), 4).

[11] Schanz and Hosius (1914–35), 1/1.5.

said. In fact, though, Funck professed a certain interest in Latin as a dead language as well. "It may be worth the trouble," he observes in what would be the final installment of his work, "to examine closely the Latin language in its deceased and mortified condition at some later date; but now, following our established order, to examine its aged decrepitude."[12] Indeed, Funck spoke more explicitly of plans for two further volumes, one examining the period of moribund latinity that extended in his view from the accession of Louis the Pious to the fifteenth century, the other treating of the modern period during which time (as Funck puts it) latinity was "reborn of heavenly goodwill towards arts and letters, revived or even summoned back from hell."[13] Not merely death, then, but rebirth figured into Funck's conception of Latin culture after Charlemagne. This rebirth is not figured as explicitly Christian: that would have been difficult, in as much as the period during which, according to Funck, the Latin language lay truly dead and buried coincides with the Christian Middle Ages, while the resurrection of latinity occurs in parallel with the rebirth of pagan antiquity. Where Isidore was happy to view in biblical terms the mixing of Latin with barbarian speech, Funck participates in the modern tendency to exorcise Judeo-Christian elements from Latin culture: his imagery thus hints at Orpheus as much as or more than at the risen Christ. But Orpheus' harrowing of hell was spectacularly unsuccessful, and the renascence of Latin culture was similarly troubled by intimations of mortality.

Soft bastard Latin, or, the nineteenth century and after

For a dead language, Latin has enjoyed a rather full afterlife. It is a pity that Funck's own death prevented him from describing it; any historian so devoted to a metaphor as he was to that of the linguistic life cycle would surely have had a lot of interesting things to say on the topic. But then again, one has to wonder how closely attuned he was to the pecu-

---

[12] *extinctam atque mortuam Latinam linguam posthac, iam uero, ut ordine progrediamur, decrepitam senectutem perlustrare, operae pretium fuerit,* Funccius (1720–50), 7: 3.

[13] *coelesti numine literis et artibus fauente resuscitatam uel ex orco reuocatam latinitatem,* Funccius (1720–50) 7: praef.

liar status that Latin attained as a dead language. When he wrote about the glorious rebirth of latinity, Funck gave no indication that he regarded that rebirth as a momentary occurrence that would give rise to yet another run of decline. Rather one expects that the pattern of death and rebirth Funck had in mind would have been something like the restored golden ages envisioned since Virgil as permanent establishments impervious to change. The perfected condition of latinity was probably something of which he felt himself to be a part, and which he expected to continue indefinitely. And why not? Even a century later the early science-fiction writer Jules Verne could peer yet another hundred years into the future and make Michel Dufrénoy, the hero of his futuristic novel *Paris in the Twentieth Century*, a prize-winning Latin poet.[14] Michel is of course a cultural relic whose prize wins him more ridicule than admiration in a world that forces poets and artists to serve the Muse in clandestine ways. Even so, it seems quaint that Verne made his hero a latinist. The decision probably reflects a realization, felt vividly a hundred years ago, that the forces of modernity (forces linked in the novel with the Americanization of French culture in general) had already begun finally to erode the privileged position of classical learning. Even Funck, who had lived to witness some of the *querelle des anciens et des modernes*, might have realized that the honored position enjoyed by Latin as a reborn classical tongue had already reached its zenith, and that its rebirth would from his time on be regarded as a temporary event or as an illusion, and that it was as a "dead language" that Latin would come to occupy its distinctive position in modern culture.

This is very different from saying that Latin is without a place in modern culture. Over the past two centuries Latin culture has experienced yet another of its periodic bifurcations, similar to the ancient divisions between classical and vulgar Latin or, later, classical and medieval Latin and, still later, between Latin and Romance. In this latest change, Latin became on the one hand part of the (*ex hypothesi*) unified academic discipline of classical philology and, on the other, a much more generally diffused part of the cultural landscape available in various ways to the learned and the unlearned to do with as they chose.

[14] The novel was written in 1863, but remained unknown until the publication of Verne (1994) (English translation 1996).

This bifurcation was hardly visible at the time when the young F. A. Wolf matriculated at the University of Göttingen in 1777, declaring himself a student of philology, but his choice of field itself was symptomatic of the coming division: at that time classical studies, and especially Latin, was so deeply ingrained in the elite educational systems of all European countries as the matrix of all other learning that to declare an intention to study it *per se* must have seemed bizarre.[15] As we can easily see in retrospect, however, Wolf set in motion a process of professionalization and segregation of the new profession from society at large that has had decisive consequences for the position of classics in contemporary culture. Like classical and medieval culture as a whole, Latin remained an element of the modern imaginary, one that developed over time, sometimes in predictable ways, sometimes not, sometimes with reference to the academic discipline, sometimes ignoring the discipline in favor of ideas that classicists viewed – and in many cases continue to view – as alien or irrelevant to their professional concerns.

The bifurcation of Latin culture in modern times can be described in terms of related discourses. One of these discourses works to deemphasize continuities and establish distinctions between kinds of latinity that would be embodied in the structure of the several academic disciplines concerned with Latin studies. This I shall regard as the esoteric discourse of latinity. It is in a way cognate with the thinking of Dante in distinguishing sharply between Latin and vernacular culture. Alongside it is a discourse in which Isidore would feel at home, but in which latinists themselves seldom if ever participate – not, at least, in their professional capacity. It thrives, however, among poets, novelists, essayists, and to an extent among practitioners of other academic disciplines as well. Within this, the exoteric discourse, a much broader view of latinity is taken, one that alternately emphasizes and disregards the distinction between kinds of latinity, between Latin itself and its Romance "daughter" languages, one that uses the Latin language, and indeed the entire language group that it persistently designates as "Latin," as an emblem for a certain set of traits that it takes to represent Latin culture as a whole.

---

[15] On Wolf and his significance as the founder of classical philology as an academic discipline, see Grafton, Most, and Zetzel (1985), 3–40 (with further bibliography, 249–54).

There are many points of contact between the two discourses, but it is convenient to begin with the familiar issue of gender. I have suggested that assumptions about the masculine gender of Latin are tested and in part redressed by developments during late antiquity and the Middle Ages, the periods during which substantial texts written by women begin to appear. As any medievalist will affirm, the tables are not turned decisively. In absolute numbers, men greatly outnumber women in the Latin culture of the Middle Ages; and ultimately, with the "rebirth of learning" and the rise of the vernacular, the idea of Latin as a language of men returns.

By the nineteenth century, Latin becomes an emblem of the intellectual accomplishments to which women aspired in vain. Consider this passage from *Little Women* (1869): " 'You needn't be so rude, it's only a "lapse of lingy," as Mr. Davis says,' retorted Amy, finishing Jo with her Latin." Here a common Latin tag is figured as male speech (attributed to Mr. Davis) disfigured in female usage by ludicrous assimilation to the vernacular; but it is still recognized as Latin and, like a magic charm, it retains its power to humble those against whom it is pronounced. Later on, Beth is asked by Frank, who will eventually marry her sister Meg, to talk to him – a simple request, but one that stymies "bashful Beth": "If he asked her to deliver a Latin oration, it would not have seemed a more impossible task." To drive this point home, later in the novel Beth looks on with admiration as the future husband of yet another sister, the aforementioned Amy, performs this very act: "Whatever his motive might have been, Laurie studied to some purpose that year, for he graduated with honor, and gave the Latin oration with the grace of a Phillips and the eloquence of a Demosthenes, so his friends said."[16] (I note in passing that Laurie's excellence is measured against the standard set by two masters not of Latin, but of English and Greek oratory.)

The impression made by such passages in popular fiction is confirmed by journalistic accounts. As the *Century Magazine* reported in an article on "Women who go to college":

The story of the progress of the education of women, even in the most favored portions of the world, is one of strange reluctance to

[16] Alcott (1869) ed. Anderson (1994), 64, 347.

97

give any advantage to the sex. Many of us have been taught to point to the inhabitants of New England as examples of remarkable care for education ... but we forget that their schools were not for women. They thought that education was something adapted to fit a boy to be a minister, or to prepare him for some other liberal calling; but as for mothers and sisters, they might still sit and spin, they might embroider and cook, they might read and write (if they did not print anything), but as for looking into a work on science, or a book in Latin or Greek, that could hardly be imagined.[17]

Classical learning long remains the popular emblem of real educational distinction, and women eventually make strides: by the end of the nineteenth century, equal educational opportunity is more accessible to women. Nevertheless we find that some girls who learn Latin experience a certain sense of gender transgression and contrast their studies to stereotypical sorts of feminine behavior. Winifred Margaretta Kirkland, an early twentieth-century memoirist, writes that

I found myself at a great city school, I a shy little country waif, most curiously clad.... I here confess that I never should have learned Latin rules if I had been prettily dressed. I wanted to show those stylish misses that there was no backwoods brain under my backwoods hat – that was all! I attributed to others a snobbishness wholly my own, and for that once clothes came perilously near costing me all human joy in human friendship. If my wardrobe had never bettered, I might now be a female Diogenes – and incidentally have furnished meteoric display for a dozen universities. My clothes improved; I am not friendless, but dull and illiterate, and all through the shaping destiny of dress.[18]

Despite this comical perception of dissonance between Latin studies and feminine behavior, girls do begin to learn Latin in greater numbers. One might even speak of the progressive feminization of Latin studies from the beginning of the century onwards. It is notable, however, and lamentable that this reorientation of gender runs in parallel with a sharp decline in the prestige of Latin studies within contemporary culture. So precipitous is that decline that by the early twentieth century other dis-

[17] Gilman (1888), 714.   [18] Kirkland (1918), 96–97.

enfranchised groups begin to disdain openly this badge of elite learning. Here is the educator Booker T. Washington, complaining about the construction of a new building at Howard University, an all-black institution: "Every man laying brick on this building was white, every man carrying a hod was a negro. The white man, in this instance, was willing to erect a building in which negroes could study Latin, but was not willing to give negroes a chance to lay the bricks in its walls."[19] Some have criticized the practical focus of Washington's educational philosophy for setting limits to black ambition, but his attitude towards the value of learning Latin agrees with what many had been saying for some time. Here is Kirkland again: "In our sane moments we perceive as clearly as does the most modern pedagogue that Greek and Latin are impedimenta to retard the boy of to-day in the race set before him, and we agree with the publisher-purveyors to youth that the compendia of useful knowledge furnished by them offer the handiest possible canned nutriment for a period that has time only for acquisition, not for digestion."[20] Kirkland is writing satirically; but Herman Melville could more seriously praise the practical arts of supposedly primitive peoples to the latinist's disadvantage: "Now, one of the peculiar characteristics of the savage in his domestic hours, is his wonderful patience of industry. An ancient Hawaiian war-club or spear-paddle, in its full multiplicity and elaboration of carving, is as great a trophy of human perseverance as a Latin lexicon." It should be understood that the narrator of *Moby-Dick* does not mean merely to praise the capacity of these "savages" by comparison with the universally recognized accomplishments of philologists. The point of the passage is to praise the art of scrimshaw: "As with the Hawaiian savage," Ishmael notes, "so with the white sailor-savage."[21] The art of the sailor's leisure time thus stands at the point of a triangle defined by the Hawaiian woodcarver on one side and the lexicographer on the other. In light of the novel's prevailing ideology, the comparison may be felt to render implicit, adverse judgment on the latinist's craft.

The tendency to measure the capacities and aspirations of women and people of color in terms of the universal language of the Euro-American elite is perhaps not surprising. What may be surprising is the

---

[19] Washington (1912), 48; cf. Washington (1903), 455.
[20] Kirkland (1918), 273–74.   [21] Melville (1851), 270.

affinity that members of that elite see between latinity and otherness. This perception is clearest in the writings of Englishmen who were particularly conscious of a linguistic and cultural difference between themselves and speakers of the Romance languages. The attitude might be expressed as a matter of sincere appreciation, as in Byron's praise of Italy:

> I love the language, that soft bastard Latin,
> Which melts like kisses from a female mouth.   *Beppo* (1818), st. 44

The string of associations that Byron evokes – bastardy, femininity, luxuriant eroticism – define the opposite qualities that members of the nineteenth-century English elite tended to see in the exotic "Latin races." He is, to be sure, writing about Italian, not Latin; but his designation of Italian as "bastard Latin" works in two opposing directions and involves the construction both of latinity itself and of the Romance languages.

Here scholarship decisively influenced the popular imagination. In 1786 Sir William Jones announced in his Third Anniversary Discourse to the Asiatic Society of Bengal that the relationship among Greek, Latin, and Sanskrit was "so strong indeed, that no philologer could examine them all three without believing them to have sprung from some common source, which, perhaps, no longer exists."[22] He further opined that Gothic, Celtic, and Persian belonged to the same "family" of languages. Jones' formulation is conventionally regarded as the originary moment of comparative linguistics. Before that time the relations among the various languages of the world were obscure; in the years that followed, the stemmatic elaboration of language "families" was carried on at a furious pace, and from linguistic structures were drawn sweeping cultural inferences as well. As one scholar has noted, "attention to culture even more than to language is found in the first work of the acknowledged founder of comparative Indo-European linguistics, Franz Bopp, as well as in that of Jacob Grimm ... [whose] *Geschichte der deutschen Sprache* (1848) would today be considered a work devoted to ethnography."[23]

Thus in the nineteenth century the linguistic division of the European nations is often figured as a binary difference between two "races," the

---

[22] Jones (1807), III.34.   [23] Lehmann (1995), 135.

Germanic and the Latin. Before comparative linguistics, it was possible for a German speaker such as Leibniz to regard Latin as the language of a culturally united Europe. A century later, some scholars might still feel this way; but increasingly Germans would regard themselves as dwelling on the periphery of this Europe and would regard Latin as a foreign tongue. The English, who for the purposes of this kind of ethnography were regarded as "Anglo-Saxons," occupied a position akin to that of German-speakers as against speakers of Romance. Discussions of this dichotomy regularly use the word "Latin" just as Byron does in the passage quoted above to designate the cultural Other in ways that suggest that the ancient origins of the "race" are never far from the writer's mind. Consider this glimpse into the future, set in the year 2000 but published in 1894:

> English, as we have seen, is already the language of 600,000,000 people, and the number is constantly increasing through its adoption by the numerous races of India, where, even before the close of the last century, it was about as important as Latin during the greatness of Rome, and by the fact that the Spanish and Portuguese elements in Mexico and Central and South America show a constant tendency to die out, much as the population of Spain fell from 30,000,000 to 17,000,000 during the nineteenth century. As this goes on, in the Western hemisphere, the places left vacant are gradually filled by the more progressive Anglo-Saxons, so that it looks as if the study of ethnology in the future would be very simple.[24]

The author of this essay in demographic extrapolation perished aboard the *Titanic*, and so did not live to see how ludicrously wrong his prophecy was, even if its linguistic point (so far) continues to hold water. But the perceived difference between "progressive Anglo-Saxons" and the "Latin race" was a commonplace idea at the turn of the century, always expressed in terms that linked language to culture and modern "Latins" to their ancient "ancestors."

So powerful was this theme of racial and cultural difference (and so convincingly was it "demonstrated" by the contrasting political

---

[24] Astor (1894), 74. For Astor's general opinion about classical education see p. iii. On p. 307, however, his protagonists encounter a spirit who communicates with them in Latin as well as English!

fortunes of Victorian England and the other European nations) that it was even embraced by some intellectuals among the "Latin peoples." Here is Gustave Le Bon writing in his influential 1896 treatise on mob psychology:

> The fundamental characteristics of the race, which constitute the unvarying source from which all our sentiments spring, always exert an influence on the irritability of crowds, their impulsiveness and their mobility, as on all the popular sentiments we shall have to study. All crowds are doubtless always irritable and impulsive, but with great variations of degree. For instance, the difference between a Latin and an Anglo-Saxon crowd is striking. The most recent facts in French history throw a vivid light on this point. The mere publication, twenty-five years ago, of a telegram, relating an insult supposed to have been offered an ambassador, was sufficient to determine an explosion of fury, whence followed immediately a terrible war. Some years later the telegraphic announcement of an insignificant reverse at Langson provoked a fresh explosion which brought about the instantaneous overthrow of the government. At the same moment a much more serious reverse undergone by the English expedition to Khartoum produced only a slight emotion in England, and no ministry was overturned. Crowds are everywhere distinguished by feminine characteristics, but Latin crowds are the most feminine of all. Whoever trusts in them may rapidly attain a lofty destiny, but to do so is to be perpetually skirting the brink of a Tarpeian rock, with the certainty of one day being precipitated from it.[25]

Just as latinity's loss of prestige eventually associates it with women, blacks, and primitive cultures, so here among the European nations Latin "races" are endowed with the qualities of the undifferentiated feminine Other.[26] Later Le Bon derives the passivity of the Latin peoples from their distinctive system of education – "very properly qualified as Latin" – which, he states, "transforms the majority of those who have undergone it into enemies of society." He quotes "a former Minister of

[25] Le Bon (1896), 21; cf. 40.

[26] For a contemporary account of the differential construction of femininity in the "Latin" and "Anglo-Saxon" cultures, see Gorren (1894).

Public Instruction, M. Jules Simon," for the opinion that "Learning lessons, knowing by heart a grammar or a compendium, repeating well and imitating well – that is a ludicrous form of education whose every effort is an act of faith tacitly admitting the infallibility of the master, and whose only results are a belittling of ourselves and a rendering of us impotent." He further associates this system of Latin education with those of China and India – playing the Orientalist card – as against those of the Anglo-Saxon nations – namely England and the United States – "who rule the world by their force of will, their initiative, and their spirit of enterprise."[27]

In this last passage, Le Bon seems to overlook the fact that Anglo-American intellectuals made Latin the basis of their elite education; and it is certainly paradoxical that they should have done so while at the same time looking with such condescension at the "Latin" peoples, those who spoke languages that were in fact descended from the ancient tongue that they so fetishized. On the other hand, one should recall the persistent theme in Latin culture of correction from outside the community of native speakers.

In the wake of the Reformation, the anglophone's sense of superiority to the Romance speaker was compounded by the religious factor. Part and parcel of the effeminacy, sensuality, and irrationality of the "Latin" peoples was their devotion to the Roman Church. As Nietzsche wrote in *Beyond Good and Evil*, "It seems that the Latin races are far more deeply attached to their Catholicism than we Northeners are to Christianity generally."[28] Edith Wharton is equally direct: "Perhaps no Anglo-Saxon fully understands the fluency in self-revelation which centuries of the confessional have given to the Latin races...."[29] Time after time, anglophone writers use the Latin language, often in a corrupt condition, as a defining symptom of Catholicism. Sir Walter Scott:

> The hermit, after a long grace, which had once been Latin, but of which original language few traces remained, excepting here and there the long rolling termination of some word or phrase, set ex-

---

[27] Le Bon (1896), 85–89. On the relationship between classical education and the French revolution see Le Bon (1913), 148–49, 186; on French versus English and American forms of democracy, (1913), 314–15.

[28] Nietzsche (1886/1909–13), XII.68.

[29] Wharton (1906), 181.

ample to his guest, by modestly putting into a very large mouth, furnished with teeth which might have ranked with those of a boar both in sharpness and whiteness, some three or four dried pease, a miserable grist as it seemed for so large and able a mill.

Ivanhoe 1.244

Here again the same views expressed by anglophones with respect to the "Latin" peoples can be found in the writings of free-thinkers within the Romance countries. Those faults that Le Bon found with "Latin education" the economist Michel Chevalier sees as part of a conspiracy involving the Church:

> An education based on the study of Latin made perfect sense in the Middle Ages. The Catholic Church had guarded preciously this heritage of the Roman empire as a symbol of unity, as a token among its members, as a private idiolect.... It must be admitted that a very great concession is made to the clergy in allowing Latin to serve as the basis of education. The clergy know Latin as well as the University; it is their own tongue. Their tuition, moreover, is cheaper; hence they must inevitably draw a large portion of our youth into their small seminaries and their schools of a higher grade.[30]

Finally, the anglophone view that the Romance languages are a debased form of the ancient, classical tongue finds its counterpart in speakers and admirers of Romance who claim for their own languages and for the universe that they describe an absolute superiority to the linguistic universe of the ancients. Thus are the traditional methods of Latin education, which are still advanced by some as the most powerfully beneficial contribution that the language can make in the modern world, derided by some champions of the vernacular:

> [The young student's] tender memory must be loaded with ablatives, conjunctions, conjugations. The blossom of human life is sacrificed to the metaphysical jargon of a dead language. What Frenchman could submit to the torture of learning his own in that manner? And if there be those who have exercised such laborious patience, do they speak better than persons who have never endured such drudgery? Who writes best, a lady of the court, or a pedantic grammarian?

[30] Chevalier (1843), 48, 52; my translation.

This indignant outburst concludes, predictably enough, with the idea that the great writer is a natural genius perfectly at home in his own language. The examples cited are telling:

> It would be easy to demonstrate that the most celebrated writers, in every walk of literature, never were brought up at college, from Homer, acquainted with no language but his own, down to J. J. Rousseau, who was a very indifferent Latin scholar.[31]

There is no need to multiply the evidence. Many of the attitudes illustrated by these passages seem humorous. They should also be familiar because some of them are still with us. For the latinist, such material is easy to ignore on the grounds that the study of Latin itself, whether among classicists, medievalists, or in any other branch of Latin studies, has nothing to do with the ill-informed notions that have prevailed in modern times. But this position is untenable. To cite only one example, but that from the founder of classical studies in America on a model adapted directly from Germany, B. L. Gildersleeve himself has been shown to have combined love and admiration for Greek culture with a visceral prejudice against "the Latin race" and Latin studies in equal measure. Not only are his attitudes a matter of record, but he took professional measures to implement them as well.[32] In more general terms it is not clear that the principles by which Latin studies has been structured are entirely uncontaminated by such thinking. I opened this chapter by observing that the sharp distinction between the classical and medieval periods is arguably the most pernicious obstacle to understanding Latin studies as a unified field. The traditional structures of Latin literary history certainly reinforce this distinction; and, in their designation of postclassical latinity as debased, corrupt, substandard, weak-minded, and generally unworthy of notice, these structures work to precisely the same ends as the sexually, racially, and religiously chauvinistic attitudes of nineteenth-century ethnography.

Is there life after death?

Ask a linguist to define the term "dead language" and you will get an answer something like this: a language whose last native speaker has

---

[31] Saint-Pierre (1836), 125–26.   [32] Habinek (1998).

died. That sounds pretty straightforward. And the issue of linguistic death is not something to be taken lightly: the number of languages in the world today that are considered moribund is large and getting larger.[33] It is a matter of speculation whether the metaphorical parallel between biology and linguistics that we unconsciously invoke whenever we speak of "dead languages" or "language families" goes deeper; but among botanists and zoologists, the decrease in global biodiversity that results when individual species are wiped out is widely viewed as a matter of serious concern. In the linguistic sphere, on the other hand, a smaller number of languages will not result in less biological raw material from which may be found new cures for disease, new opportunities to understand the workings of our own bodies, the origins and the ends of life on our planet. Arguably, the loss of linguistic diversity tends in the other direction: when everyone speaks English (since this seems at the moment to be the direction in which we are heading) there will be fewer barriers separating those who may collaborate on producing the benefits that could come from the study of the Earth's fewer and fewer remaining forms of life. But it is difficult, I should think, for any philologist not to feel a sense of loss at the death of a language. Just as Latin killed off its neighbors, so English is now threatening to kill Welsh, Cornish, Scots, and Irish. It has already killed and continues to kill any number of North American languages. Even in India, where fifteen other official and hundreds of unofficial languages are spoken, the prevalence of English, to say nothing of its power and prestige, is such that it can hardly be considered a foreign tongue any longer. It is overwhelmingly likely that all over the world the number of languages that die because the children of their native speakers become native speakers of English will continue to increase. In this sense, the death of a language is not a metaphorical but a real event, and is in some ways as tragic as any death.

Let us accept, then, that a language can die. We may still ask: Is Latin in fact dead? Is death necessarily forever? Is there an afterlife? Or, can a dead language ever come back to life?

Most linguistic revivals, however dramatic, involve endangered rather than dead languages. Many European languages facing death

---

[33] On dead and endangered languages see Robin (1993), Robins and Uhlenbeck (1991), Dorian (1989).

have been made the focus of nationalist preservation movements, and some of those mentioned above as endangered languages, along with Basque, Catalan and a few others, have lately shown stronger life signs. A language considered dead can nevertheless serve a political purpose even if no thought is given to revival. Indeed, for an emerging nation-state, gaining possession of a dead language can be almost as advantageous as reviving a dying one, and it is certainly a lot less trouble; it is rather like coming into an unexpected inheritance instead of making money oneself. The founder of the modern Turkish state, Kemal Ata-türk, encouraged secular and western social principles by breaking with many traditions of the recent Islamic past and claiming Turkish descent from the Hittites, with corresponding claims for the status of Hittite as a dead, classical language. Conversely, the British discovery of Sanskrit tested jingoistic assumptions about the superiority of their culture to that of India: it was troubling to people like Thomas Babington Macaulay, Whig historian and author of the *Lays of Ancient Rome*, that these colonized "orientals" possessed a classical language that was not only cognate with, but more ancient than both Latin and Greek.[34] Later, when India gained its independence, Sanskrit was seriously proposed as the official national language; its "classical" status and associations with cultural ascendancy in the distant past placed it conveniently above regional identity politics.[35] And ancient Greek was seriously proposed as the official language of the fledgling United States of America.

The prize for actually reviving a dead language, however, goes to Hebrew – or would, except for the fact that speakers of that language do not really want the prize on these terms. Hebrew, it is argued, never actually died because there has been a continuous and unbroken tradition of using Hebrew from antiquity down to modern times. The language therefore underwent a renascence, but this was possible only because it was not entirely dead. The facts are as follows. By the Renaissance, Hebrew had certainly attained classical status and was confined mainly to texts. As a spoken language, it began to decline as early as the sixth century BC as Jewish communities adopted Aramaic,

---

[34] For Macaulay's role in the Anglicist-Orientalist controversy, see Kopf (1995), especially 146–49.

[35] Ramaswamy (1994).

Greek, Latin, and other tongues. By the second century AD this process was probably complete. For the next eighteen hundred years no one conversed in Hebrew, except under unusual circumstances; no one came by it naturally as his or her first language; no one used it for commerce, social intercourse, or other quotidian purposes. It was almost exclusively a sacred and a scribal language, sanctified by the holy scriptures that were written in it and employed by scholars who studied and explicated those scriptures for one another. When it was heard it was in the form of recitation and not of spontaneous conversation. It continued in this state until the birth of the Zionist movement in the late nineteenth century, when it began to be spoken and adapted to the purposes of modern life.[36]

With few alterations, of course, precisely the same things might be said about Latin. Like Hebrew, Latin has been in continuous use since antiquity. Long before the Renaissance children had ceased to come by Latin naturally as their first language. It enjoyed a special status as a sacral language, sanctified by holy scriptures. It was employed by scholars who studied and explicated those scriptures for one another. It was often heard in the form of recitation of traditional texts. But by comparison with Hebrew, Latin actually possessed more of the characteristics associated with a living language. Its use extended to many areas of scholarship, science, culture, diplomacy, medicine, law, and commerce as well. Though largely confined to elite circles, the number of people who used it was much larger than the community of those who used Hebrew. The members of this Latin community included women as well as men, while the woman who knew Hebrew was an extreme rarity. Unlike Hebrew, Latin was by no means an exclusively written language, but was used extensively for conversation. During the early modern period and for many years thereafter Hebrew led an extremely tenuous existence while Latin flourished in ways that make it indistinguishable from a living and indeed thriving language. And yet it is Hebrew today that has been reborn, while Latin is thought dead, even paradigmatically dead – the deadest of all dead languages.

Is Latin then simply different from Hebrew? Did Latin in fact die while Hebrew was secretly thriving, biding its time until its dramatic, Zionist rebirth? Another way of asking this question is, could Latin be

---

[36] Fellman (1973), 11–17.

similarly reborn? Merely to pose the question is to invite ridicule. There does not exist, nor can one imagine there will ever be within Latin culture the political will necessary to accomplish a linguistic miracle like the revival of Hebrew. The Church, of course, controls its own state, still uses Latin extensively, and has even since 1953 put out a periodical, *Latinitas*, which is devoted to the use of Latin in the modern world. But no one will mistake the Holy See for the state of Israel, linguistically or otherwise. Enthusiasts, of course, there are and will always be. They form an interesting set of subcultures consisting mostly of people who are not professional latinists; but at least some professionals do see these groups as a rewarding place to spend their off-hours, and it may be that all latinists should pay more attention. The interests of these people include Latin conversation and the promotion of international languages based on Latin. Related to this activity is a fairly large bibliography of items advocating the revival of Latin as an international language.[37] But however interesting this activity may be, it does not suggest that Latin is about to rise from the dead.

A fascinating instance of the ways in which the professional discourse relates to that of the enthusiast emanates from the remarkably active Latin industry that is based in Finland. Since 1989, the Finnish Broadcasting Company (YLE) has been producing "*Nuntii Latini*," a weekly radio news summary in (*sic*) "classical Latin." One result of this effort is that there exists a chronicle of recent history written in Latin consisting of program transcripts published in three volumes, with a fourth in progress. Two members of the broadcast team teach Latin at Helsinki University. The University of Jyväskylä boasts a faculty member in the Department of Literature who moonlights by performing "traditional Finnish tangoes" and rock-and-roll music, including several songs by Elvis Presley, translated into Latin by a colleague in the Department of Latin; the latter also has plans to do live Latin commentary on a hockey game. In June 1997, the same university hosted the Nonus Conventus Internationalis Academiae Latinati Fovendae, a society that promotes (among other things) conversational Latin. What, we may ask, is going on here?

Is there some sort of intrinsic connection between the high profes-

---

[37] Constructed languages based on Latin in whole or in part include Novilatin, Nov Latin, Semilatin, Interlingua, LSF or "latino sine flexione," SPL, and Esperanto.

sional standards of Finnish latinists (all of the latinists mentioned above have distinguished publication records) and their desire to belt out "Quate, Crepa, Rota" ("Shake, Rattle, and Roll")? Are both their professionalism and their enthusiasm for the *patrius sermo* related to the fact that their "mother tongue" does not belong to the Indo-European family? One hesitates even to venture into this territory without the company of a skilled sociolinguist. It does, however, seem clear that these efforts generate interest beyond the immediate circle of enthusiasts chiefly because they are so very improbable: the very idea of hearing Latin on the radio, an ancient language known only to a relative few broadcast over a modern medium of mass communication, is a kind of *adunaton*, not the shape of things to come.

If Latin really *is*, in contrast to what speakers of Hebrew maintain about their own "mother tongue," a "dead language" – whatever that may mean – then I would not hold out much hope for "revival." Lucretius, as we have seen, equated the specifically latinate verbal texture of his poem on nature with the underlying structure of nature itself. It therefore seems reasonable, in considering the possibility of linguistic rebirth, to invoke his views on the possibility of actual rebirth. Even if, Lucretius says, over the course of limitless time, in the vastness of limitless space, the very same atoms that now comprise one's body and soul should come back together in the same combination and position as they are now found, and were to create creatures who looked and acted exactly like ourselves, they still would not *be* ourselves; for they would lack one essential ingredient, *repetentia nostri*, the memory of our self-hood, which would be dissolved and irretrievably lost at our death (*DRN* 3.847–51). The linguist's view of linguistic death is like this: once the continuity of native speakers learning the language from their elders is finally broken, the language is dead, and cannot be revived. Whatever is created out of the atoms of the dead language may resemble it, but cannot be identical with it.

What this may or may not imply about the status of other languages I leave to others to decide. In the case of Latin, I believe it suggests without question that whatever of the language has died, is dead and is destined to remain so. This dead language is not wholly inaccessible: many scholars have worked hard and well to recover some sense of living Latin idiom through the philological method. Nevertheless, I think one must admit that the keen refreshment that one's sense of latinity receives from hard-won philological insight into the workings of the living language in and of itself suggests chiefly how much more must have been lost. There remains a sense in which no modern person can viscerally understand the Latin of the past. And beyond this, there are simple, obvious impossibilities: we will never savor the sound of Laelia's voice; we will never cringe at the accents of Arrius or Valerius Soranus. We may consider carefully what Cicero and Quintilian mean when they praise speech that is *tersus, pressus, urbanus*, we may even feel that we can intuit exactly what these words connote, but we will never hear Latin spoken that way or speak it ourselves; and however well we may know the learned language, our knowledge can never be informed by contact with the living speech of antiquity, of the Middle Ages, or of most of the period since the Renaissance.

But beyond this, I would suggest that questions about "revival" are irrelevant. It is useless to say that Latin died with its last native speaker. In a practical if mundane sense, our knowledge of linguistic history at this level is insufficiently detailed to determine who in, say, the third, fifth, or seventh century may or may not have been a "native speaker" of Latin. On a more theoretical plane, I have tried to show that the concept of "native speakers" of Latin is highly problematized by the widespread, ages-old tendency to imagine the language almost exclusively as a highly constructed cultural artifact. There was, one has to assume, a sense in which Latin was once someone's "mother tongue," and this language is indeed dead to us. But beside this language was a latinity to which one was never born, but which one always had to acquire. In this respect Dante was not entirely wrong, nor is the modern philologist guilty of mere pedantry when invoking the idea of "loan words" between vulgar and classical Latin speech. We are clearly dealing with what has always been a culture of diglossia. Sometimes the two registers, the natural and the cultural, verge closely upon one another. Quintilian at the beginning of his treatise takes pains to ensure that the highly constructed speech of the elite will be as natural as possible for the rising young orator, that it will if possible replace for him the vulgar tongue entirely: that he may regard any nativisms in one's latinity as flaws needing to be purged; that he may, like Atticus at Arpinum, find anyone's affection for the things to which he was born, no matter how attractive, just a bit strange. Quintilian's Latin program is less a matter of teaching the future speaker a grammar-chastened version of his native speech as a second language than of limiting all contact with the vulgar speech of untutored contemporaries to the furthest possible degree; and so effective was the institutionalization of cultured latinity that about the vulgar tongue we really have only the slightest information. What we know of it is mainly confined to some of the ways in which it differs from the elite dialect and how it resembles what would eventually become Romance. Whatever further data we may acquire can tell us only about its corpse, not its living essence.

The situation of the language that has survived is entirely different. This language died not with its last "native speaker," but has been in continuous use since antiquity. It is not an exclusively scribal language, but has at times been widely spoken as well. Its "death" is hardly a matter of falling into disuse as a previously unbroken tradition ended with the disappearance of a community of qualified users. It is constructed in our histories as a simple matter of writers straying farther and farther from the "norm" represented by a particular (and none-too-rigorously defined) chronological period. Moreover, and by the same reasoning, its "rebirth" involved nothing more than a return to this norm. According to this view, the "death" and "rebirth" of a language is a totally bloodless affair. It is a matter of learning and acculturation – of imitating the correct models in the correct way. So long as the exemplars survive, latinity may lie dormant, but it can never die: revival is an ever-present possibility.

Viewed in this light, the principles by which the most influential histories of latinity structure themselves, together with the notion that Latin was or is a "dead" language, are revealed as the merest of metaphorical constructs possessing limited basis in reality or explanatory power. The time may be at hand, not to revive the language, but to replace the metaphors.

5

The voices of Latin culture

Dead language, dead metaphor

The Latin language has developed not in a series of horizontal periods stacked like uniform blocks in a simple pattern of rise and fall, but in strands now running in parallel, now intertwined, some broken and some continuous, from antiquity down to today. It is a language like any other, historically unique but nevertheless subject to the same general laws that govern all languages. The metaphors that have been used to understand it – metaphors of "gold," of "death," metaphors involving tax-brackets, blocks of time, gender, and authority – have largely lost their exegetical power and by now do as much to obfuscate the social and cultural dimensions of latinity as ever they did to clarify and explain. Latin studies needs new metaphors and needs to employ them cautiously, more cautiously than it did the old. Some lie ready to hand, but little used. Others can be invented and then discarded as needed. The point will be not to establish a new standard, but to work with a sense that the new metaphor is never more than just a metaphor, and to prevent any merely metaphorical construct of literary history from assuming in one's mind the status of an independent reality.

While a certain set of metaphors has indeed come to dominate institutional thinking about latinity, how many latinists are really happy with them today? Yet these metaphors continue to trouble the unconscious mind of Latin studies; or, if that seems too extravagant, then let us just observe that they have not yet been discarded or replaced. In the previous chapter I attempted to make a case against these metaphors by examining their relevance to a particular (now long past) set of historical circumstances and suggesting their general irrelevance to the challenges and opportunities facing Latin studies today. In this final chapter, I will try to revive a few other metaphors that have occasionally informed thinking about the language and, in conclusion, to suggest one that I believe holds promise as a means of organizing Latin studies on a more open and inclusive model. To repeat, this is by no means an effort to establish a new orthodoxy. In fact, I would argue that in the current intellectual climate both within Latin studies and at large, orthodoxy is neither possible nor desirable. I would further argue that allowing Latin studies to remain structured according to an outdated orthodoxy in which no one any longer really believes is one of the few remaining obstacles to a real explosion of creativity in the field, which has already in the past few years shown real and remarkable signs of new intellectual vitality.

The old metaphors will never disappear. The idea of a golden age is one that recurs throughout the history of Latin letters. Attention to this motif certainly ought to inform one's thinking about Latin culture. The problem is when students of Cicero, Catullus, Livy, and Ovid begin to think of their "period" of literary history as *the* golden age and do not think about what this term means, why it was applied to this period, whether it makes sense to view it as a period, and how it stands in relation to other golden ages, like those of Charlemagne or of Petrarch. A related problem exists when anyone unreflectively thinks of Latin as a "dead language," as I have tried to suggest in the previous chapter. One corrective for this problem involves not the simple-minded insistence that "Latin lives!" but rather interrogation of the metaphor itself in relation to others that have informed thinking about the language.

"Not dead, but turned to stone"

In this connection, the metaphor of stone might seem an unpromising one, suggesting nothing so much as the continued debasement that follows gold and silver past bronze and iron, itself perhaps to be followed in turn by dust. We think inevitably as well of the "stone age," hardly an attractive comparison or one that seems adequate to describe any period of Latin culture. But periodization is not the point. The metaphor of the stone language has been used in various ways to describe the beauties of Latin speech. One of the most enthusiastic examples comes from the pen of none other than renegade classicist Friedrich Nietzsche.

Better known of course as a philosopher and as a hellenist than for his work on Roman topics, Nietzsche nevertheless admired Latin for its expressive power.[1] In *Twilight of the Idols* there is a chapter entitled "Things I owe to the Ancients," and the first point he addresses is the development of his distinctive style:

> My sense of style, for the epigram as style, was awakened almost spontaneously upon my acquaintance with Sallust. I have not forgotten the astonishment of my respected teacher Corssen, when he was forced to give his worst Latin pupil the highest marks – at one stroke I had learned all there was to learn. Condensed, severe, with as much substance as possible in the background, and with cold but roguish hostility towards all "beautiful words" and "beautiful feelings" – in these things I found my particular bent. In my writings up to "Zarathustra," there will be found a very earnest ambition to attain to the *Roman* style, to the "*aere perennius*" in style. The same thing happened upon my first acquaintance with Horace. Up to the present no poet has given me the same artistic raptures as those which from the first I received from an Horatian ode. In certain languages it would be absurd even to aspire to what is accomplished by this poet. This mosaic of words, in which every unit spreads its power to the left and to the right over the whole, by its sound, by its placement in the sentence, and by its meaning, this *minimum* in the compass and number of the signs, and the *maximum* of energy in the signs which is thereby achieved – all of this is Roman, and, if you will believe me, noble *par excellence*. By the side of this all the rest of poetry becomes something popular – nothing more than senseless sentimental twaddle.[2]

The motif of the stone language as deployed by Nietzsche is hardly revolutionary: the qualities of solidity and tangibility that he imputes to the language are commonplaces. But the two contrasting associations of

---

[1] Nietzsche's endorsement of Latin prose-composition exercises can be found in the essay "Human, all-too-human" (1878/1909–13), VI.185–86.

[2] Nietzsche (1889/1909–13), XVI.112–13.

stone – of stone monuments, and of stone *tesserae* in a mosiac pattern – have been developed by others, independent of Nietzsche, in excitingly different ways.

According to Michael Roberts, a predilection for certain rhetorical figures, images, and allusive procedures can be understood as comprising a distinct and coherent approach to Latin poetics, an approach that he calls "the jeweled style."[3] Roberts situates this style in the poetry of late antiquity, specifically from the time of Ausonius to that of Venantius. As he notes, however, the basic elements of the style – patterning, careful repetition, equally careful variation; correlation between the visual placement of words on a page and the visual images that the words often describe; a cunning development of metapoetic language – can be found in the Latin poetry of earlier (and, though Roberts does not explicitly make this point, later) times. It is the metaphorical material of this metapoetic language that changes most through those times: Roberts convincingly correlates the imagery of the Neoteric garland with that of gemstones in the language of formal rhetoric and literary criticism, discussing important instances of jewel imagery in the poetry of Maecenas (fr. 2 Morel–Büchner) and Martial (5.11.3–4) as well as in Tacitus (*Dial.* 22.4). In the process, he opens up the possibility of tracing new lines of influence by stressing the importance of Catullus and especially Lucretius rather than Virgil as the chief classical analogues of this late antique style.[4] What is most liberating about this treatment, however, is Roberts' own treatment of metaphor, both the development of a metaphor that was already part of the latinist's critical vocabulary and a willingness to, as it were, mix metaphors, or to treat metaphors as such rather than mistaking them for facts and allowing them to limit and restrict the ideas to which they refer. Stones are hard and durable like granite; but they are bright and colorful like flowers. This is a singularly apt language for describing poetry that is so brilliant and has proven so durable.

The connection between Nietzsche and Roberts through the metaphor of stone affirms that the critical imaginary of Latin culture is

---

[3] Roberts (1989); see especially chapter 2, "The literary tradition and its refinement," pp. 38–65.

[4] Any effort to investigate further the principles of Roberts' "jeweled style," particularly repetition, has now been greatly facilitated by the appearance of Wills (1996).

already larger and more various than is sometimes recognized. No existing history of the Latin language or literature has been written in such terms as these; but individual latinists do think in these terms, and in doing so they describe (and participate in) a culture richer and more diverse than can be found in standard reference works, one structured by connections that cross the traditional boundaries of period and place, style and substance. The metaphor of stone is but a small instance of the surprising explanatory power of an unfamiliar trope and also of the tenacious grip of the old. When one first encounters the metaphor in Nietzsche it inevitably conjures up some very traditional and rather staid associations. Only when one is reminded that a jewel is also a stone does the metaphor take on a more radiant quality, and it becomes possible to think of Latin as an expressive medium that is like both granite and diamonds.

Even without turning granite into diamonds, however, one can read the metaphor of stone in surprising ways. The image reappears in Igor Stravinsky's characterization of Latin as "a medium not dead, but turned to stone, and so monumentalised as to have become immune to all forms of vulgarization."[5] Thus did the composer explain his decision to use a Latin libretto for his 1927 opera/oratorio *Oedipus Rex*. The production of this libretto was a complicated matter. It began as a French text by Jean Cocteau – a different one from his *Oedipe-roi*, very different from *La Machine infernale* – that was then translated into Latin by his friend Jean Daniélou. This libretto evidently involved considerable revision under Stravinsky's influence: Cocteau's script itself went through several drafts in French, and we have documentary evidence of the composer's imperious demands that his collaborator make repeated changes, bearing in mind that his words would eventually be translated into Latin – a prospect that did nothing to increase Cocteau's enthusiasm for the project. Thus it is clear that the idea of a Latin text was integral to Stravinsky's conception, since extracting a suitable one from his collaborators was such a complicated matter.

As Stravinsky wrote to Cocteau, his aim was to create "an opera in Latin based on a universally known tragedy of the ancient world."[6] The selection of Sophocles' *Oedipus Tyrannus* as a starting point is

---

[5] Stravinsky (1936), 125.
[6] *Per litteras* Oct. 11, 1925; see Craft (1982–85), I.94–95.

immensely interesting in terms of modernist esthetics. On the one hand, it was Freud who relatively recently had canonized this play as the definitive version of the most universally important myth not only of Greek antiquity but in human consciousness itself. In this sense Stravinsky's choice was as inevitable after Freud as it would have been unthinkable before. But in other respects Stravinsky's fellow modernists regarded the *Oedipus* as a betrayal.[7] Certainly the choice of Latin instead of Greek for the libretto requires explanation, not least because it runs somewhat counter to well-known preferences that Stravinsky, a titanic figure in the modernist movement, might have been expected to share.

But it was in large part the idea of a Latin text itself that appealed to Stravinsky. Even the status of Latin as an ecclesiastical language did not trouble him; indeed, it was a positive attraction. Certainly the idea of a concert-length work in Latin, particularly one with a movement entitled "Gloria," invites comparison with musical settings of the Roman Mass. Further, though Stravinsky as we shall see minimizes the importance of this fact, his Latin librettist Daniélou was a twenty-year-old student who later went on to a distinguished career in the Church and was eventually elected cardinal.[8] The composition of the *Oedipus* also coincides with Stravinsky's return to Christianity, a development that gave rise to the idea "that a text for music might be endowed with a certain monumental quality by translation backwards, so to speak, from a secular to a sacred language."[9] Monumentality is here linked with the sacred as previously with immunity to vulgarization. On this point, Stravinsky is especially interesting:

> I sometimes read in program notes that the language of my *Oedipus* is "medieval Latin," a rumor no doubt derived from the fact that my translator was a Catholic cleric. But the Latin, judging by the sentence structure, the placement of modifiers, and the use of the historical infinitive, is Ciceronian. I have found only one "ecclesiastical" word in the whole libretto, and that – the *omniscius pastor* – can be called such only by association. (*Why* the shepherd should be omniscient I do not know.) Unusual grammatical situations can be

[7] Walsh (1993), 17.   [8] Walsh (1993), 99–100 n. 16.
[9] Stravinsky and Craft (1963), 4, 9.

found – for example, the ablative form *"Laudibus Regina,"* which Daniélou may have borrowed from an old text – but they are rare. Idiomatically, the language is all pre-Boethian. But the Latinist is horrified by the first letter of my score, the "K," which does not exist in the language he knows. The purpose of this barbarian orthography was to secure hard, or at least non-Italianized, sounds instead of the usual potpourri of classic and ecclesiastic ...

My scansion is entirely unorthodox. It must break every rule, if only because Latin is a language of fixed accents and I accentuate freely according to my musical dictates ...[10]

There are at least two possible reactions to all of this. One of these is that the libretto, as a piece of latinity, is a disaster and the composer's linguistic commentary on the text an embarrassment. Even if we allow for the caginess with which artists habitually discuss their work (he does not *know* why the shepherd should be *omniscient*?), Stravinsky's efforts here to explicate his text seem to indicate about the level of familiarity with Latin that one would expect in an eighty-year-old man who had not studied the language for years.

The composer's insistence that his text's latinity is classical and not medieval or ecclesiatical is striking – all the more so in light of his reference to Latin as a "sacred language." In any case, citing the historical infinitive as a characteristically ciceronian construction is bizarre, and the assertion that the entire libretto is "idiomatically pre-Boethian" is wrong, meaningless, or perhaps both. It is of course an obvious fact that the Latin of the *Oedipus*, far from being in the pure, classical idiom that the author claims, is actually a monstrous hybrid. Anxious to insure a hard, classical "c" or "k" sound in performance (which he represents also as an effort to avoid contamination of Latin speech by allowing it to become "Italianized"), Stravinsky showed no similar concern about the semivowel "u," which he wrote as "v" and which is regularly pronounced in performance as is the English "v." In addition to the *omniscius* we find *miki* for *mihi*, an apparent medievalism that Stravinsky, however, explains as an orthographical error imported from his own Russian transliteration. Thus, by employing his eccentric orthography, Stravinsky distances his libretto's Latin from Italian, but assimilates

[10] Ibid., 14–15.

it to Russian. Along with *ecce* appears the subclassical (or, certainly, unciceronian) *ellum*. One could cite many other sins against standard latinity. Consider for instance this passage from the first act:

> ŒDIPUS   Non reperias vetus skelus,
> Thebas eruam.
> Thebas incolit skelestus.
>
> CHORUS   Deus dixit, tibi dixit.
>
> ŒDIPUS   Tibi dixit.
> Miki debet se dedere.
> Opus vos istum deferre.
> Thebas eruam,
> Thebis pellere istum,
> Vetus skelus non reperias.
>
> CHORUS   Thebis skelestus incolit.
>
> ŒDIPUS   Deus dixit ...
> Sphynga solvi, carmen solvi,
> ego divinabo,
> Iterum divinabo,
> clarissimus Œdipus,
> Thebas iterum servabo.
> eg' Œdipus carmen divinabo.
>
> CHORUS   Solve! Solve, Œdipus, solve!
>
> ŒDIPUS   Polliceor divinabo.
> Clarissimus Œdipus,
> polliceor divinabo.

Translators have done their best with this passage, of which Stravinsky himself observed that "the grammar, and therefore the meaning, is obscure ... I no longer possess a copy of the French text, and I can only guess at the original meaning."[11] *Thebas eruam* is usually rendered "I will search the city thoroughly," as if Latin possessed the English idiom "I will turn Thebes upside-down." Without the original French, as Stravinsky notes, it is hard to know what gave rise to this odd Latin

---

[11] Stravinsky and Craft (1963), 15.

usage. *Non reperias vetus skelus* is variously rendered as "You cannot right this ancient wrong," "Du wirst dieses alte Verbrechen nicht wiedergutmachen," and "On ne peut réparer la vielle offense." Here the French translation, though it is not Cocteau's original script, but a translation back into French from Daniélou's Latin, may well give us a clue, namely, that the Latin translator mistakenly used *reperire* instead of *reparare*. Beyond observing that he has lost Cocteau's French original of the libretto, Stravinsky does not comment on any further illegitimate influences from modern languages on Daniélou's Latin; but he does worry about perfectly legitimate influences from another quarter. For the usual Greek accusative *Oedipoda* alongside the latinized *Oedipodem* Stravinsky suggested the unnecessary correction *Oedipum*. Can we relate this misguided impulse towards hyperlatinism with a certain anxiety about the relationship between Latin and Greek? "I used Latin rather than Greek," Stravinsky admits, "because I had no notion of how to treat Greek musically (or Latin, Latinists will say, but there I did at least have *my* idea)." With these and many other points that I have not cited, Stravinsky supplies ample ammunition to the professional latinist who wishes to convict him of ill-informed pretension and intellectual fraud. This is the reaction that Stravinsky obviously expects and perhaps experienced in academic circles.

The other possible reaction, and the one that I personally favor, is to avoid this rush to judgment and to assess the position of this text not in terms of its adherence to some timeless standard, but as a document of contemporary latinity. As with any work of art, the question ought to be not merely *is* the Latin ciceronian or not, but what does it *mean* that a twentieth-century author *claims* this status for it? Clearly neither Cicero himself, nor any contemporary of Cicero's, nor anyone sufficiently well trained in and seriously committed to the canons of "classical" latinity would have been capable of producing a text like this and calling it ciceronian. It is possible but, I submit, irrelevant that Stravinsky may have been deceived about the highly idiosyncratic latinity of his text. It is obvious on the other hand that the ciceronian standard was of great symbolic importance. The canonization of Cicero as *the* standard by which all latinity should be measured marks the real beginning of the Neo-Latin period, of that linguistic afterlife during which Latin became the paradigmatically dead language; but Stravinsky salutes Cicero while explicitly rejecting the dead metaphor. "Not dead, but turned to stone, and so monumentalised as to have become immune to all forms of vulgarization." This too is ironic, whether intentionally or not, in that Stravinsky's Latin text is in fact replete with deliberate departures from classical norms as well as simple errors in typography, spelling, diction, grammar, and syntax. All of these might reasonably be considered symptoms of "vulgarization," of an infection that contaminates pure latinity with the taint of the substandard, of the nonclassical, of the vernacular. Stravinsky takes a different view: the value of a Latin text consists in the fact that it is *by definition* "immune to all forms of vulgarization." Even if the librettist must, for instance, resort to "barbarian orthography" to insure accurate pronunciation, introducing one form of vulgarization in order to prevent another, the text as a whole rises above these epiphenomena, resisting vulgarization as a whole simply because it is in Latin.

This kind of symbolic significance would have been practically unavailable in any other linguistic medium. The mere fact that the text is in Latin and insists on its status as a Latin text associates it with other documents of canonical latinity that have been regarded as embodying the qualities of timelessness, immutability, and so forth. It is equally clear that the text desires to access various other qualities – a sacral tone, an almost primitivist esthetic – that one does not associate with classical latinity, but with the Latin of earlier or later periods. Many passages of the *Oedipus* sound less like any product of the classical period than they resemble such fossilized (turned to stone?) specimens of deep antiquity as the Song of the Arval Brethren on the one hand, or musical relics of the medieval Church (on this rock?) on the other. These associations were apparently easier to acquire than the association with classicism, upon which Stravinsky therefore had to insist. His claim is to this extent paradoxical, in that the norms of classical latinity are very much at odds with the more various and "debased" latinity of other times; and yet in Stravinsky's view these incompatible elements are held in suspension within his text by the single medium of the Latin language. Historically, Latin had in fact contained all these diverse elements; consequently, it carries in its stream all the conflicting associations that the composer wished for his libretto. To condemn either the latinity of this work or the composer's treatment of it would be a superficial and self-defeating judgment. The libretto of Stravinsky's *Oedipus* is no academic exercise in prose composition, but a work of art. It is one of the most notable and creative engagements with the Latin language produced in this century. What sort of latinist would be content simply to judge such a work unworthy of acknowledgment or notice?

As important as this *Oedipus* is to modern Latin artistry, Stravinsky's commentary is an equally important contribution to the history of ideas about the language. His austere, but liberating formulation – "a medium not dead, but turned to stone" – neutralizes the most prevalent and unhelpful metaphor encumbering the language and replaces it with one that has a significant if unappreciated history of its own; and at the same time, by his practice he refuses to be constrained, but elects to be empowered by the new metaphor in his effort to revive latinity as an artistic medium for the modern world.

The image of a stone language is a radically overdetermined characterization of latinity. For this very reason it is a useful place to begin discussing alternative metaphors for latinity; but for the same reason, it cannot take us very far. We may remember this metaphor, perhaps even cherish and develop it; but it should not be allowed to inhibit the search for others.

Different tongues

The diversity of Latin speech is a theme congenial to the postmodern condition. Instead of a language that silences all others, Latin is better appreciated as one among many. Instead of a language realized ideally in the stylistic preferences of one author or one historical period, it is appreciated as richer and more appealing for the diversity that it gained through time and space in the contrasting voices of many speakers. This is a theme, I suggest, that merits further exploration. Whether it could lead to a new history of latinity, a history that emphasizes the play of voices against one another, always and everywhere, rather than attempting to construct successive, homogeneous periods of better or worse latinity according to ideas of rise and fall, death and rebirth, I will not guess. Historical consciousness remains, and will remain, an indispensable element of Latin studies, but synchronicity has its place as well. In any case, the long sweep of Latin culture need not be divided into so many discrete epochs before we can say anything about it.

The project of reimagining latinity along these lines is long, even indefinite; but this book is drawing to a close. Let me conclude with a text that self-reflexively draws upon the dialogical resources of latinity to present itself as an image of linguistic, musical, and cultural polyphony. One might find such a text within the ancient canon, but in the spirit of crossing old boundaries, let me move beyond the pomerium of the classical period and consider the social and cultural dimensions of the language in a period when its power, far from growing, as it was in Virgil's day, was under pressure from developments that it could not control, ones that would eventually demote Latin to its current position of marginality among world languages.

The English Renaissance might seem a paradoxical moment in which to seek this different perspective. This was, after all, a time when humanist learning, aided by the rediscovery of Greek, was reforming the "debased" latinity of the Middle Ages on a more classical model. This was a time when Latin, even if it was nobody's "mother tongue," was nevertheless a living language. Indeed, we have recently been shown that Latin culture during the sixteenth and seventeenth centuries in England alone attained a depth and diversity that is difficult to comprehend, flourishing alongside the new vernacular culture to an extent that challenges familiar notions about relations between social and intellectual history during the period.[12] The material that was produced is voluminous and diverse. It includes poetry of many genres on both classical and biblical themes; drama; biography; treatises on literary theory, philosophy, sports, education, law, theology, music, and other topics; translations from Greek, Hebrew, and the vernacular. At the same time, it is perhaps too easy to err in the opposite direction and to assume that the place of Latin culture was actually more secure than it really was. The vernacular would after all prove much too powerful for Latin to survive in anything like the richness and diversity that it briefly attained. It would be better to think of Latin as the language of a kind of subculture, were it not for the fact that the members of this culture were all securely placed in the top tier of English society. Perhaps a useful comparison is with the francophone Russian aristocracy of the nineteenth century – though that culture produced nothing like the range of literature in French that Renaissance England produced in Latin. And of course in a certain sense no change took place at all, in that Latin was merely replaced by another prestige dialect, as Antonio

---

[12] For a survey of this material see Binns (1990).

Gramsci has observed in respect to the rise of modern Italian. Those in positions of power and privilege tended to remain the same, regardless of what linguistic heraldry they wore.

It is against this background that I wish to close this essay. I want to imagine a time when the success of Latin culture was largely in the past and the pressures and anxieties it faced had less to do with world dominion and more with mere survival. The totalizing discourse of the Roman empire was inherited by the Roman Catholic Church of the Middle Ages, an institution that was perhaps less utterly dominant than is sometimes popularly imagined, but one that nonetheless stood as the single most powerful and longest-lived social, political, and intellectual force that the west has ever seen. Indeed, its power is still great. But since the Reformation it has never been the temporal force that it had been.

One of the most interesting moments in the history of latinity is when Latin ceased to be the language of an all-powerful, pan-European institution and found itself in the unfamiliar position of being the speech of the oppressed. This actually happened in England when a law was passed forbidding the use of Latin for worship in all but a few cases. The most important composer of this time was Thomas Tallis, honored in later times almost as the original voice of English musicianship.[13] But Tallis speaks in many voices. For composers of his time, the issue of earning one's livelihood was intimately bound up with the politics of religion and of language.

In 1547, Tallis' place of employment, the Chapel Royal, became a Protestant establishment. Until that date it had, of course, been a seat of Catholicism. Its musical culture had exhibited the characteristic features of Catholic worship: a fetishistic devotion to the cult of the Virgin; a highly sophisticated range of choral styles; and, naturally, the almost exclusive use of Latin as a liturgical language. But with the accession of Edward VI, all of this changed almost overnight. Not only was Latin banned, but a general revulsion from "popery" led to simplifications in almost all matters of cult, including a simpler musical style: what would be the point of worshiping in the vernacular if musical intricacy rendered the hymns unintelligible? Catholic worship returned with Queen Mary in 1553, but Elizabeth abolished it again for good in 1559.

[13] On Tallis' life and works see Doe (1980).

Throughout this period composers found themselves in a tricky situation. To adapt to the changing styles favored by patrons in a spirit of mutual rivalry and innovation had long been a part of the musical culture of Catholic Europe, including England. But to do so in context of deadly religious warfare was another matter.

Different men coped with the problem in different ways. Nicholas Ludford, until that time a prolific and much-admired composer just then at the height of his powers, fell silent, producing no new music under the Protestant regime. William Byrd, on the other hand, produced vast quantities of music for the Anglican liturgy; but he also published separately a collection of Latin masses and votive pieces for the private, and probably clandestine, use of those who clove to the Roman Church.[14] Tallis was Byrd's teacher and, later, his senior colleague at the Chapel Royal. Like Byrd, he negotiated with great aplomb the conflicting demands of his profession and his faith by adapting his languages to shifting ideological situations. It is easy to assume that proficiency in diverse tongues was one of the chief lessons that Byrd learned from his master.

In closing, let us examine one of Tallis' compositions in some detail. The piece I have in mind is a setting of a New Testament text, Acts 2 : 4 and 11, in paraphrase:

> et repleti sunt omnes Spiritu Sancto
> et coeperunt loqui aliis (uariis AI*c*) linguis
> prout Spiritus Sanctus dabat eloqui illis ...
> audiuimus loquentes eos nostris linguis magnalia Dei.
>
> > Biblia Vulgata

And they were filled with the Holy Spirit, and began to speak in other (various) tongues, just as the Holy Spirit granted them the ability to do ... We heard them speaking in our own languages about the great things of God.

(chant)	Loquebantur	a
(polyphony)	uariis linguis apostoli, alleluia,	B
	magnalia Dei,	C
	alleluia.	D

---

[14] On Catholic elements in Byrd's music see Monson (1997), with further references.

(chant)	Repleti sunt omnes Spiritu Sancto,	e
	et ceperunt loqui	
(polyphony)	magnalia Dei,	C
	alleluia.	D
(chant)	Gloria Patri et Filio et Spiritui Sancto,	f
(polyphony)	alleluia.	D

Tallis' adaptation

The apostles spoke in various tongues, alleluia, about the great things of God, alleluia. They were filled with the Holy spirit, and began to speak about the great things of God, alleluia. Glory to the Father and to the Son and to the Holy Spirit, alleluia.

The text concerns the first Pentecost, a day after the ascension of Jesus into heaven when the twelve apostles were huddled in fright in the upper room of a building – the same room in which they had taken the Last Supper, and in which the risen Lord had appeared to the eleven, and after that to Thomas. On this day, "a sound as of violent wind approaching came suddenly from the sky and filled the whole building where they were staying; and there appeared to them individual tongues as of fire, and settled upon each of them. And they were filled with the Holy Spirit ..." The apostles go forth from the room and speak in diverse tongues to the multinational, polyglot group assembled in Jerusalem.

The feast of Pentecost celebrates the origin of Christianity as a religion of polyglossia. The main theme of Acts is, of course, the development of Christianity from a renegade Judaic sect to a new religion independent of national boundaries. The chapter on which Tallis draws represents this development as the result of an originary linguistic miracle. The apostles – like Jesus, Jews, and unlike Paul, who emerges as the hero of Acts, unschooled in the international Hellenistic culture of the first-century Mediterranean – speak Aramaic, which has been aptly described as the *lingua franca* of the old Persian empire. They are thus ill-equipped to take Jesus' Gospel to the West, an area firmly under the cultural hegemony of Greece. But the miracle that then occurs predicts the future career of Christianity. "Filled with the Holy Spirit," they find themselves able to address the international multitude assembled in Jerusalem with confidence, with authority, and in the correct language.

It is in fact notable that the Holy Spirit in this story is very closely identified with polyglossia. The apostles huddle in the upper room afraid and monoglot. The Holy Spirit descends upon them in the form of "tongues" of flame. (The Vulgate reads *linguae*, the Greek text γλῶσσαι.) They emerge from the room to address boldly a notably polyglot audience. The text is insistent upon this last point. The homes of those present are listed in a catalogue that runs to some eight lines and limns a linguistic map of the Mediterranean basin from Parthia to Rome – the two great military and political powers of the period. The "route" followed by the catalogue predicts the route that the apostles themselves, and particularly the hellenized Paul – a native of Tarsus and a *civis Romanus* – were to take in bringing the Gospel to the West. For this to occur not only courage was needed but fluency in many languages as well. The apostles received both under the guise of the Holy Spirit. The passage of Acts that commemorates this event understandably became a traditional part of the Pentecost liturgy; and appropriately, Tallis' setting of the text emphasizes its celebration of linguistic multiplicity.

The musical form that Tallis uses is known as a responsory or, in England, a respond. This form embodies the concept of multivocality in two ways. First, it incorporates polyphony, with different vocal lines moving simultaneously but independently of one another. Second, the respond often begins, as this example does, with a single voice and develops by alternating sections of plainchant with polyphony. This contrast throws the elaborate polyphony into high relief against a comparatively subdued background. I would also note that, as the name "respond" suggests, the form derives its power both from the repetition of a single musical setting of a specific portion of the text and, in this case, from the dialogue between sections of plainchant and polyphony "answering" one another.

The dialogic structure of the respond possesses a further dimension in that it reflects the historical development of religious music in Christian Europe. Like many other sacred forms, the respond borrows its basic musical material from the vast repertory of plainchant that was the chief element of almost all liturgical usage throughout the Middle Ages. Polyphony developed after about the eleventh century, first in the practice of composing melismatic counterpoint to traditional plainchant, which for this purpose was sung in a style that involved holding each note of the chant for extended periods of time (a role assigned to the "tenor" voice; hence our modern terminology), and, eventually, in the development of a mature polyphony in which all voices make approximately equal contributions to the overall texture of a piece. In many forms of this mature style, particularly in settings of the Mass, it was customary to precede a polyphonic composition with a line of the traditional plainchant setting of the text: so the alternation in Tallis' respond between the composer's polyphony and the traditional Sarum material on which it is based.[15]

Beyond its observance of typical respond structure, Tallis' setting sensitively emphasizes the polyglossic nature of the text. Section a consists of a single word (*loquebantur*, "they were speaking") and is assigned to a single voice that sings the Sarum melody. This is a perfectly conventional feature of religious music in the Renaissance. In this piece, however, convention is put to a specific use as the single voice establishes a monologic ground against which the subsequent polyphony reveals itself. But even the single voice speaks of a plurality (*"they* were speaking"). The many are implied by the one. It is this plurality that is developed and celebrated in the next section of the piece (B), which sets the words *uariis linguis* ("in different tongues"). Tallis' polyphonic style lends itself here to vivid word-painting, as two groups of three and two voices, respectively, enter one after the other on the first word, *uariis*. The different voices of Tallis' musical polyphony "are" the different voices in which the Apostles spoke. This insistence on the thematic word *uariis* ("different") is clearly motivated, but conceals an ironic subtext; for, if we refer to a critical edition of the Vulgate, we discover that *uariis* is itself a variant reading for *aliis*. It is unlikely that Tallis was even aware of this textual uncertainty; but, as if his purpose were to acknowledge the multiform history of his text, he insists on *uariis* almost as a deliberate choice, repeating the thematic word emphatically as each of five musical voices enters his composition.

The Vulgate's *aliis* represents with arguably greater accuracy than *uariis* the reading of the Greek text, ἑτέραις, a fact that points to a third element of latent polyglossia in the text. The Latin of the Vulgate, or of the medieval tradition that derives from the Vulgate, is not in any sense original. It is, as its name implies, a popularization or even a debase-

---

[15] Sarum Chant is the body of plainchant, related to Gregorian Chant but musically distinct, associated with the liturgy at Salisbury (*Sarisberia*) from 1078–1547; details in Berry (1980).

ment of a more ancient and authoritative Greek text. With the next word of the respond, *apostoli* – that is, ἀπόστολοι – a Greek word surfaces in the Latin text.[16] ἀπόστολος is a very conventional Greek word used in the classical period to denote messengers, emissaries, and so forth. There are Latin words that express the same ideas, such as *nuntius*, *legatus*, and the like. But the Greek word underwent a history not unlike that of the synonymous ἄγγελος, a more common word for messenger used in the Septuagint to translate the Hebrew *mal'akh* and then used especially to denote "a messenger from God" – not any human or inanimate messenger, but a whole class of beings whose existence is entirely hidden from human intelligence in the normal course of events. Similarly, ἀπόστολος came to denote the emissaries charged with spreading Jesus' teachings. In Greek it remained possible to speak of human ἄγγελοι and conventional ἀπόστολοι, but in Christian contexts, the words would carry special meanings. Latin, however, was able to borrow the words as *angelus* and *apostolus*, which have become the English "angel" and "apostle." In a sense, then, the Latin text appeals to the sacral authority of its Greek exemplar.[17]

The first polyphonic section continues by venturing into new linguistic territory, which is marked by the Hebrew word "alleluia." Having begun in Latin and moved on through Greek (*apostoli*) to Hebrew in this way, the respond moves back through the three sacred languages of the crucifix inscription as defined by Isidore, performing in miniature the linguistic journey of St. Willibald from Heidenheim to the Holy Land and back as described by Reginold of Eichstatt in a tenth-century poem that begins in Latin, changes to Greek, then to Hebrew, then back to Greek and finally Latin again, paralleling the stages of Willibald's journey.[18] Our text is not quite that ambitious; but having encompassed

[16] Note also the contrasting musical treatments of *uariis linguis* and *apostoli*. Where five successive voices enter on the first phrase in imitative fashion, the harmonic texture changes suddenly on the second phrase as all voices enter simultaneously, but with very independent melodic lines: thus the musical setting deepens the sense of different voices. I owe this observation to Cristle Collins Judd.

[17] For Greek as a sacral language in Latin culture see Kaimio (1979), 162–67 (who deals only with pagan Rome) and Berschin (1988), 18–26 (for the Christian Middle Ages).

[18] Discussed by Berschin (1988), 173–74, with further references.

the three sacred languages in its first two sections, one of plainchant and one of polyphony, it has not quite finished its own glossolalia.

Before we consider sections C and D (*magnalia dei, alleluia*, "the great things of God, alleluia"), which will be repeated in their entirety, let us skip briefly ahead to the text that intervenes between the two appearances of this phrase (section e). This text is set as straight chant and equally straight Latin: *repleti sunt omnes Spiritu Sancto, et ceperunt loqui ...* ("They were filled with the Holy Spirit, and they began to speak about ..."). The mystical event is tersely described, but Tallis' arrangement is artful in that it leads the listener back in a ring. The first chant section (a) had consisted of a single word, *loquebantur*; this section (e) is longer, but concludes with another form of the same word, *loqui*. We thus see that the chant sections, a and e, are a narrative setting, and that the polyphonic sections represent the inspired utterance of the pentecostal moment. Further, while the chant sections are utterly pure in their latinity, the polyphony adds Greek and Hebrew too: polyphony is revealed as polyglossia. So far each successive section of the respond has glossed or completed the sense of what preceded it, and this pattern continues – not just in a syntactical sense, but symbolically as well. At this point one might misconstrue the linguistic symbolism of the piece, understanding univocal Latin to be contrasted with polyphonous Greek and Hebrew. But the recurring textual and musical material that surrounds this second plainchant text (sections C and D) causes us to understand the symbolism of Latin polyphony in a different way.

The Latin Bible does not simply mine the Greek for loan words that become part of its sacred technical vocabulary, but actually follows it in constructing such words. "The apostles related in diverse tongues *the greatnesses* of God." An outlandish translation is called for here: the Latin has <u>*magnalia Dei*</u>. No classical author ever used a word like *magnalia*. Its basic meaning is obvious, and in formation it is, clearly enough, a very common adjective, *magnus* ("large, great"), with an adjectival suffix, *-alis*. *Magnalia*, being the neuter plural form, must mean "great things," but must also be distinguished somehow from the conventional Latin equivalent of that phrase, which is simply *magna* (as in the text of the "Magnificat": *quia fecit mihi <u>magna</u>, qui potens est*, "For he that is mighty has done *great things* to me"). This difference I have inadequately suggested by the coinage "greatnesses"; but to understand it fully, we must go back again to the Latin, and then to the Greek.

As I have mentioned, no classical author uses the word *magnalia*; in fact, this is the only occurrence of the word in the New Testament. It occurs twenty-one times in the Old Testament, and is used by several Christian writers as well, who seem to have picked it up from scripture. In fact, the passage from Acts is sufficient to put us on the right interpretive track if we consult the Greek: ἀκούομεν λαλούντων αὐτῶν ταῖς ἡμετέραις γλώσσαις τὰ μεγαλεῖα τοῦ Θεοῦ (2 : 11), "we hear them telling in our own languages of *the greatnesses* of God." The Greek word μεγαλεῖα is in form precisely similar to the Latin *magnalia*. It, too, is nothing more than the conventional word for "large" or "great" (μέγας) supplied with an adjectival suffix. It, too, is a neuter plural form meaning "great things" that must somehow be distinguished from the normal sort of great things (τὰ μέγαλα). And, like *magnalia*, it is very uncommon outside the Bible. No single word is its counterpart in Hebrew; rather it seems be a specifically Greek verbal instantiation of a Jewish theological concept, "the great things of God." μέγαλα evidently seemed inadequate to express this idea, so μεγαλεῖα and then *magnalia* were invented. To this idea in its distinctive lexical form, *magnalia Dei*, followed by the Hebrew word *alleluia*, Tallis devotes sections C and D of his composition, with voices soaring and intertwining: the three sacred languages rise above their human condition and become as a mystical, multivocal whole. The Latin text becomes more than the ground against which Greek and Hebrew establish conditions of heteroglossia: rather, Latin is revealed as inherently dialogical in its relationship to different tongues.

The piece ends quietly, with a plainchant doxology (f) and a second polyphonic alleluia (D); and I will end quietly too, stepping back inside the classical pomerium, just to see how things look there after this excursion. Or better, how things sound. The voices are familiar, but they sound a bit different, no?

Varietas enim Latinum uerbum est, idque proprie quidem in disparibus coloribus dicitur, sed transfertur in multa disparia: uarium poema, uaria oratio, uarii mores, uaria fortuna, uoluptas etiam uaria dici solet, cum percipitur e multis dissimilibus rebus dissimilis efficientibus uoluptates.

"Variety" is a Latin word and is properly used of different colors, but metaphorically of many differences: one speaks of a varied poem, a varied speech, varied character, varied fortune, even of varied pleasure when one feels different pleasures from the effects of many different things.   Cicero *Fin.* 2.10

Appendix: Nepos fr. 59 in the edition of Marshall (1977)

Verba ex epistula Corneliae Gracchorum matris ex libro Cornelii Nepotis de Latinis historicis excerpta:

"Dices pulchrum esse inimicos ulcisci. Id neque maius neque pulchrius cuiquam atque mihi uidetur, sed si liceat re publica salua ea persequi; sed quatenus id fieri non potest, multo tempore multisque partibus inimici nostri non peribunt atque, ubi nunc sunt, erunt potius quam res publica profligetur atque pereat."

Eadem alio loco:

"Verbis conceptis deierare ausim, praeterquam qui Tiberium Gracchum necarunt, neminem inimicum tantum molestiae tantumque laboris, quantum te ob has res, mihi tradidisse; quem oportebat omnium eorum, quos antehac habui liberos, partis eorum tolerare atque curare, ut quam minimum sollicitudinis in senecta haberem, utique quaecumque ageres, ea uelle maxime mihi placere, atque uti nefas haberes rerum maiorum aduersum meam sententiam quicquam facere, praesertim mihi, cui parua pars uitae restat. Ne id quidem tam breue spatium potest opitulari, quin et mihi aduersere et rem publicam profliges? Denique quae pausa erit? Ecquando desinet familia nostra insanire? Ecquando modus ei rei haberi poterit? Ecquando desinemus et habentes et praebentes molestiis desistere? Ecquando perpudescet miscenda atque perturbanda re publica? Sed si omnino id fieri non potest, ubi ego mortua ero, petito tribunatum; per me facito quod lubebit, cum ego non sentiam. Ubi mortua ero, parentabis mihi et invocabis deum parentem. In eo tempore non pudebit te eorum deum preces expetere, quos uiuos atque praesentes relictos atque desertos habueris? Ne ille sirit Iuppiter te ea perseuerare, nec tibi tantam dementiam uenire in animum. Et si perseueras, uereor ne in omnem uitam tantum laboris culpa tua recipias, uti in nullo tempore tute tibi placere possis."

Bibliography

Adams, J. N. (1982) *The Latin Sexual Vocabulary.* London
    (1984) "Female speech in Latin comedy," *Antichthon* 18: 43–77
Alcott, L. M. (1869) *Little Women*, ed. Valerie Anderson, Oxford and New York
    (1994)
Astor, John Jacob (1894) *A Journey in Other Worlds.* New York
Auerbach, Erich (1965) *Literary Language and its Public in Late Antiquity and the
    Middle Ages*, trans. Ralph Manheim. Princeton
Bardy, G. (1948) *La Question des langues dans l'Eglise ancienne.* Paris
Barwick, Karl (1964) (ed.) *Flavius Charisius Sosipater, Artis grammaticae libri V*, 2nd
    edn. F. Kühnert. Leipzig
Berry, Mary (1980) "Sarum rite, music of the," in Stanley Sadie (ed.), *The New Grove
    Dictionary of Music and Musicians*, vol. XVI: 512–13. London
Berschin, Walter (1988) *Greek Letters and the Latin Middle Ages from Jerome to
    Nicholas of Cusa*, trans. Jerold C. Frakes, rev. edn. Washington
Binns, J. W. (1990) *Intellectual Culture in Elizabethan and Jacobean England: The
    Latin Writings of the Age.* Leeds
Bloomer, W. Martin (1992) *Valerius Maximus and the Rhetoric of the New Nobility.*
    Chapel Hill
Bodine, Ann (1975) "Sex differentiation in language," in Barrie Thorne and Nancy
    Henley (eds.), *Language and Sex: Difference and Dominance*, 130–51. Rowley,
    Mass.
Bonjour, Madeleine (1975) *Terre natale: Etudes sur une composante affective du
    patriotisme romaine.* Paris
Bowman, Alan K. and Thomas, J. David (1994) *The Vindolanda Writing Tablets.*
    London
Boyle, A. J. (1988) (ed.) *The Imperial Muse: To Juvenal through Ovid.* Monash
Broughton, T. R. S. (1951–52) *The Magistrates of the Roman Republic.* With the
    collaboration of M. L. Patterson. *Philological Monographs* no. 15, v. 1–2. New
    York
Canon, Garland and Brine, Kevin R. (1995) (eds.) *Objects of Enquiry. The Life,
    Contributions, and Influences of Sir William Jones (1746–1794).* New York

Chevalier, Michel (1843) "Rapport de M. Villemain sur l'instruction secondaire," *Journal des Economistes* 5, April–July: 23–57

Conte, Gian Biagio (1994) *Latin Literature: A History*, trans. Joseph B. Solodow, rev. Don Fowler and Glenn W. Most. Baltimore

Craft, Robert (1982–85) (ed.) *Stravinsky, Selected Correspondence*. 3 vols. New York

De Mauro, Tullio (1972) *Storia linguistica dell'Italia unita*. 3rd edn. Bari

DeJean, Joan (1989) *Fictions of Sappho, 1546–1937*. Chicago

Doe, Paul. (1980) "Tallis, Thomas," in Stanley Sadie (ed.), *The New Grove Dictionary of Music and Musicians*, vol. XVIII: 541–48. London

Dorian, Nancy C. (1989) (ed.) *Investigating Obsolescence: Studies in Language Contraction and Death*. Cambridge

Dronke, Peter (1984) *Women Writers of the Middle Ages: A Critical Study of Texts from Perpetua (†203) to Marguerite Porete (†1310)*. Cambridge

Edwards, Catharine (1996) *Writing Rome: Textual Approaches to the City*. Cambridge

Eichenberger, Thomas (1991) *Patria: Studien zur Bedeutung des Wortes im Mittelalter (6.–12. Jahrhundert)*. Sigmaringen

Feeney, Denis (1998) *Literature and Religion at Rome: Cultures, Contexts, and Beliefs*. Cambridge

Fellman, Jack (1973) *The Revival of a Classical Tongue: Eliezer Ben Yehuda and the Modern Hebrew Language*. Contributions to the sociology of language 6. The Hague

Funccius, J. N. (1720–50) *De variis Latinae linguae aetatibus*. Marburg

Gabba, Emilio (1991) *Dionysius and the History of Archaic Rome*. Berkeley

George, Judith W. (1992) *Venantius Fortunatus: A Latin Poet in Merovingian Gaul*. Oxford

Gibbon, Edward (1909–14) *The History of the Decline and Fall of the Roman Empire*, ed. J. B. Bury. 3 vols. Rpt. 1974. New York

Gilman, Arthur (1888) "Women who go to college," *Century Magazine* 36: 714–18

Godman, Peter (1987) *Poets and Emperors: Frankish Politics and Carolingian Poetry*. Oxford

Gold, Barbara K. (1993) "'But Ariadne was never there in the first place': finding the female in Roman poetry," in N. S. Rabinowitz and A. Richlin (eds.), *Feminist Theory and the Classics*, 75–101. New York

Gorren, A. (1894) "Womanliness as a Profession." *Scribner's Magazine* 15 (May 1894): 610–15

Grafton, Anthony, Most, Glenn W., and Zetzel, James E. G. (1985) (trans.) *Prolegomena to Homer, 1795, by F. A. Wolf*. Princeton

Habermehl, Peter (1992) *Perpetua und der Ägypter, oder Bilder des Bösen im frühen afrikanischen Christentum: ein Versuch zur Passio sanctarum Perpetuae et Felicitatis*. Texte und Untersuchungen zur Geschichte der altchristlichen Literatur 140. Berlin

Habinek, Thomas N. (1998) *The Politics of Latin Literature: Writing, Identity, and Empire in Ancient Rome*. Princeton

Haefele, Hans F. (1980) (ed.) *Ekkehardi IV Casus Sancti Galli/Ekkehard IV, St. Galler Klostergeschichten.* Ausgewahlte Quellen zur deutschen Geschichte des Mittelalters 10. Darmstadt

Hallett, Judith P. (1984) *Fathers and Daughters in Roman Society: Women and the Elite Family.* Princeton

    (1992) "Martial's Sulpicia and Propertius' Cynthia," *Classical World* 86.2: 99–123

Häring, Nikolaus M. (1985) (ed.) "Alan of Lille, 'De Planctu Naturae'," *Studi Medievali* 19: 797–897

Harvey, Elizabeth D. (1989) "Ventriloquizing Sappho: Ovid, Donne, and the erotics of the feminine voice," *Criticism* 31: 115–38

Hellerstein, Kathryn (1990) "Hebraisms as metaphor in Kadya Molodowsky's 'Froyen-Lider I'," in Ellen Spolsky (ed.), *The Uses of Adversity: Failure and Accommodation in Reader Response,* 143–52. Berkeley

Herzog, Reinhart (1993) (ed.) *Restauration et renouveau: La littérature latine de 284 à 374 après J.-C.* Turnhout

Hinds, Stephen (1987) "The poetess and the reader: further steps towards Sulpicia," *Hermathena* 143: 29–46

    (1998) *Allusion and Intertext: Dynamics of Appropriation in Roman Poetry.* Cambridge

Holzberg, Niklas (1999) "Four poets and a poetess, or, a portrait of the poet as a young man? Thoughts on book 3 of the *Corpus Tibullianum*," *Classical Journal* 94: 169–91

Johnson, W. R. (1976) *Darkness Visible: A Study of Vergil's Aeneid.* Berkeley

Jones, Sir William (1807) *The Collected Works of Sir William Jones.* 13 vols. Rpt. 1993. New York

Kaimio, Jorma (1979) *The Romans and the Greek Language.* Helsinki

Keil, Heinrich (1857–80) *Grammatici Latini.* Leipzig

Kenney, E. J., and Clausen, W. V. (1982) (eds.) *Cambridge History of Classical Literature.* Vol. II: *Latin Literature.* Cambridge

Kirkland, Winifred Margaretta (1918) *The Joys of Being a Woman and Other Papers.* Rpt. 1968. Freeport, N.Y.

Kollmann, E. D. (1971) "Lucretius' criticism of the early Greek philosophers," *Studii Classice* 13: 79–93

Kopf, David (1995) "The historiography of British orientalism, 1772–1992," in Canon and Brine (1995) (eds.), 141–60

Lakoff, Robin (1975) *Language and Woman's Place.* New York

Le Bon, Gustave (1896) *The Crowd: A Study of the Popular Mind.* New York

    (1913) *The Psychology of Revolution.* New York

Lehmann, Winfred P. (1995) "The impact of Jones in German-speaking areas," in Canon and Brine (1995): 131–40

Lindsay, W. M. (1913) *Sexti Pompei Festi De verborum significatu quae supersunt cum Pauli epitome.* Leipzig

Lowe, N. J. (1988) "Sulpicia's syntax," *Classical Quarterly* 38: 193–205

MacMullen, Ramsay (1966) "Provincial languages in the Roman empire," *American Journal of Philology* 87: 1–17

Malcovati, Enrica (1976) *Oratorum Romanorum Fragmenta Liberae Rei Publicae*. 4th edn. Turin

Marshall, Peter K. (1977) *Cornelii Nepotis vitae cum fragmentis.* Leipzig

Martindale, Charles (1993) *Redeeming the Text: Latin Poetry and the Hermeneutics of Reception.* Cambridge

Mazzocco, Angelo (1993) *Linguistic Theories in Dante and the Humanists: Studies of Language and Intellectual History in Late Medieval and Early Renaissance Italy.* Leiden

McKitterick, Rosamond (1989) *The Carolingians and the Written Word*

Melville, Herman (1851) *Moby-Dick, or, The Whale,* in Harrison Hayford, Hershel Parker, and G. Thomas Tanselle (eds.), *The Writings of Herman Melville: The Northwestern-Newberry Edition,* vol. VI (1988). Evanston and Chicago

Millar, Fergus (1968) "Local culture in the Roman empire: Libyan, Punic and Latin in northern Africa," *Journal of Roman Studies* 58: 126–34

Monson, Craig (1997) "Byrd, the Catholics, and the motet: the hearing reopened," in Dolores Pesce (ed.), *Hearing the Motet: Essays on the Motet of the Middle Ages and Renaissance,* 348–74. New York

Nietzsche, Friedrich (1878) *Menschliches, allzumenschliches, ein Buch für freie Geister.*
(1886) *Götzen-Dämmerung; oder, Wie man mit dem Hammer philosophiert.*
(1889) *Jenseits von Gut und Böse: Vorspiel einer Philosophie der Zukunft.*
(1909–13) *The Complete Works of Friedrich Nietsche,* ed. Oscar Levy. 17 vols. London

Nolan, Edward Peter (1994) *Cry Out and Write: A Feminine Poetics of Revelation.* New York

Norberg, Dag (1966) "A quelle époque a-t-on cessé de parler latin en Gaule?" *Annales* 21: 346–56 = *Au seuil du moyen âge: Etudes linguistiques, métriques et littéraires publiées par ses collègues et élèves à l'occasion de son 65ᵉ anniversaire* (1974): 3–16

O'Donnell, James J. (1994) Review of Herzog (1993), *Bryn Mawr Classical Review* 5.5: 415–26

Odgers, Merle Middleton (1928) "Latin *parens,* its meanings and uses," Diss. Philadelphia, University of Pennsylvania

Ong, Walter J. (1959) "Latin language study as a renaissance puberty rite," *Studies in Philology* 56: 103–24; = *Rhetoric, Romance, and Technology: Studies in the Interaction of Expression and Culture* (1971): 113–41

Parker, Holt (1992) "Other remarks on the other Sulpicia," *Classical World* 86.2: 89–95
(1994) "Sulpicia, the *Auctor de Sulpicia,* and the authorship of 3.9 and 3.11 of the *Corpus Tibullianum,*" *Helios* 21: 39–62

Paton, W. R. (1917) *The Greek Anthology.* Vol. II Cambridge, Mass. and London

Perkins, David (1992) *Is Literary History Possible?* Baltimore

Poole, Roger (1995) *The Unknown Virginia Woolf,* 4th edn. Cambridge

Ramaswamy, Sumathi (1994) "Sanskrit for the nation," Unpublished ms.

Rawson, Elizabeth (1973) "The interpretation of Cicero's 'De legibus'," *Aufstieg und Niedergang der römischen Welt* I/4: 334–56 = *Roman Culture and Society: Collected Papers* (1991): 125–48

Reeve, M. D. (1983) "Martial," In *Texts and Transmission: A Survey of the Latin Classics*, ed. L. D. Reynolds. 239–44. Oxford

Ribbeck, Otto (1897–98) *Scaenicae Romanorum poesis fragmenta*, 3rd edn.

Richlin, Amy (1992a) "Sulpicia the satirist," *Classical World* 86.2: 125–39

(1992b) "Julia's jokes, Galla Placidia, and the Roman use of women as political icons," in Barbara Garlick, Suzanne Dixon, and Pauline Allen (eds.), *Stereotypes of Women in Power: Historical Perspectives and Revisionist Views*, 65–91. New York

(1993) "The ethnographer's dilemma and the dream of a lost golden age," in Nancy Sorkin Rabinowitz and Amy Richlin (eds.), *Feminist Theory and the Classics*, 272–303. New York

Roberts, Michael (1989) *The Jeweled Style: Poetry and Poetics in Late Antiquity.* Ithaca, N.Y.

Robin, Régine (1993) *Le deuil de l'origine: une langue en trop, la langue en moins.* Saint-Denis

Robins, Robert H. and Uhlenbeck, Eugenius M. (1991) (eds.) *Endangered Languages.* Oxford

Saint-Pierre, Bernadin de (1836) *Studies of Nature,* trans. Henry Hunter. London

Salmon, E. T. (1972) "Cicero, Romanus an Italicus anceps," in John R. C. Martyn (ed.), *Cicero and Virgil: Studies in Honour of Harold Hunt.* Amsterdam, 75–86

Scaliger, Julius Caesar (1561) *Poetices libri septem*: Faksimile-Neudruck der Ausgabe Leipzig von Lyon; mit einer Einleitung von August Buck. Stuttgart 1987

Schanz, M., and Hosius, C. (1914–35) *Geschichte der römischen Literatur bis zum Gesetzgebungswerk des Kaisers Justinian.* Munich

Scioppius, Gaspar (1675) *Cogitationes de uariis Latinae linguae aetatibus.* Hafniae

Sedley, David (1998) *Lucretius and the Transformation of Greek Wisdom.* Cambridge

Seidman, Naomi (1997) *Marriage Made in Heaven: The Sexual Politics of Hebrew and Yiddish.* Berkeley

Shaw, Brent D. (1993) "The passion of Perpetua," *Past & Present* 139: 3–45

Smith, Kirby Flower (1913) *The Elegies of Albius Tibullus.* New York

Snyder, Jane MacIntosh (1980) *Puns and Poetry in Lucretius' De Rerum Natura.* Amsterdam

Solmsen, Friedrich (1986) "Aeneas founded Rome with Odysseus," *Harvard Studies in Classical Philology* 90: 92–110

Stravinsky, Igor (1936) *An Autobiography.* New York

Stravinsky, Igor and Craft, Robert (1963) *Dialogues and a Diary.* Garden City, N.Y.

Szöverffy, J. (1977) "A la source de l'humanisme chrétien médiéval: 'Romanus' et 'barbarus' chez Venance Fortunat," *Aevum* 65: 71–86

Tatum, W. J. (1984) "The presocratics in book I of Lucretius' *De Rerum Natura,*" *Transactions of the American Philological Association* 114: 177–89

Tavoni, Mirko (1984) *Latino, grammatica, volgare: Storia di una questione umanistica.* Medioevo e umanesimo 53. Padua

Verne, Jules (1994) *Paris au Xxe siècle.* Paris

(1996) *Paris in the Twentieth Century,* trans. Richard Howard. New York

Versteegh, Kees (1987) "Latinitas, Hellenismos, 'Arabiyya'," in Daniel J. Taylor (ed.), *The History of Linguistics in the Classical Period*, 251–74. Philadelphia

Walsh, Stephen (1993) *Stravinsky: Oedipus Rex.* Cambridge

Wardy, Robert (1988) "Lucretius on what atoms are not," *Classical Philology* 83: 112–28

Washington, Booker T. (1903) "The fruits of industrial training," *Atlantic Monthly* 92: 453–62

(1912) "Is the negro having a fair chance?" *The Century Illustrated Monthly Magazine* 85 (N.S. 63), no. 1, November

Wessner, Paul (1931) *Scholia in Iuuenalem uetustiora.* Leipzig

Wharton, Edith (1906) *Madame de Treymes.* New York

Wheeler, Everett L. (1988) *Stratagem and the Vocabulary of Military Trickery.* Leiden

Wills, Jeffrey (1996) *Repetition in Latin Poetry: Figures of Allusion.* Oxford

Wright, Roger (1982) *Late Latin and Early Romance in Spain and Carolingian France.* Liverpool

Yeats, W. B. (1962) *Explorations. Selected by Mrs. W. B. Yeats.* New York: Macmillan

Ziolkowski, Jan (1985) *Alan of Lille's Grammar of Sex: The Meaning of Grammar to a Twelfth-Century Intellectual.* Cambridge, Mass.

Index

CPSIA information can be obtained at www.ICGtesting.com
Printed in the USA
BVOW071216181012

303333BV00001B/4/A